TEMPLE
LEA
HOUSTON

TEMPLE LEA HOUSTON as he appeared as Senator of Texas 1885-89.
Courtesy Sam Houston Museum, Huntsville, Texas. Reproduced by
Revelle Studio, Huntsville.

Golden Heritage And Silver Tongue Of

Temple Lea Houston

by

Bernice Tune

EAKIN PRESS ★ BURNET, TEXAS

FIRST EDITION

Published in the United States of America
By Eakin Press, P.O. Drawer AG, Burnet, Texas 78611

ISBN 0-89015-282-9

Dedication

This book is dedicated to two very lovely ladies, Mrs. Mary Henderson, the youngest child of Temple Lea Houston for her devoted assistance in making this book more accurate. And to my mother, Mrs. Eula Tune, for the constant faith and encouragement in this endeavor.

ABOUT THE AUTHOR

Author Bernice Tune has been writing since a senior in high school. After having had a poem published in the local paper in Hamilton, Texas, she became more confident and began discussing this aspect of a career with her English teacher, who discouraged her from trying because the teacher knew she would not be able to attend college and felt this was necessary to becoming a good writer.

She kept writing secretly; but with no one to critique her work she eventually slacked off. During World War II she had another poem published in the base paper, which was picked up and re-published by Stars and Stripes.

She joined the Abilene Writers Guild in 1968 as a charter member and began to work and study to improve her skill. Her work has been published in *Frontier Times* and *Modern Maturity*. She has participated in all of the guilds workshops.

After graduation from high school she attended business college in Fort Worth and in recent years took writing courses taught by Juanita Zachry, International Correspondence School, Tarrant County Junior College, and an English composition course at University of Oklahoma.

The author lives with her mother at 1609 Muse, Fort Worth, Texas, works for Data Processing Security, Inc., and is a member of Brentwood Church of Christ.

CONTENTS

I.   Trial of Minnie Stacey   1

II.   Childhood of Temple Lea Houston   7

III.   College, Bar Examination   15

IV.   Romance and Marriage   19

V.   Home in Mobeetie   25

VI.   Texas Senator From The Panhandle   30

VII.   Court Trials   34

VIII. The Run, New Friends, New Life   37

IX.   Trial of a Lonely Cowboy   45

X.   A New Home in Oklahoma   51

XI.   Gunfire And Death   59

XII.   Legal Skulduggery   67

XIII. His Final Work   74

XIV. Aftermath   78

APPENDICES

Most Of Houston's Outstanding Speeches

A. Address of Temple Lea Houston, San Jacinto Battlefield, April 21, 1880 85

B. Defense of Gen. Houston 92

C. Vindication of Father as presented by E.H. Thrall in his Texas History, Nov. 4, 1880 95

D. Houston's Eulogy to Texas Heroes, Unveiling of Monument of San Jacinto, Aug. 25, 1881 100

E. Letter from R.M. Hall to Houston in response to some of Houston's questions 105

F. Nomination of Sam Bell Moxey to U.S. Senate, Jan. 26, 1887 110

G. Dedication of the Texas State Capitol Bldg, May 18, 1888 114

H. American Civilization (no date given) picture of portion of handwritten copy included........... 125

I. Dedication of Castle on the Hill, Northwestern State College, Alva, Oklahoma, July 1, 1898 134

J. Astronomy, given to group of teachers, 1897 146

K. Tennessee Centennial Address, May 1, 1897 161

L. Tribute to Temple Houston, given by Rev. Father Kamp at funeral of Houston 165

LIST OF ILLUSTRATIONS

Temple Lea Houston as he appeared as Texas
Senator 1885-89. . . . . Frontispiece
Birthplace of Temple Lea Houston,
Texas Governors Mansion in 1866. 6
Temple Lea Houston, Age 12. 12
Temple Lea Houston, Cadet at Baylor Military Academy. 14
Mrs. Laura Cross Houston, wife of Temple Lea Houston. 26
Collection of Indian Artifacts. .38, 39
Temple Houston Law Book with bullet hole, saved his life. . .50
Houston Home in Woodward, Oklahoma. 54
Letter from law partner. 60
Temple Houston about age 40. .66
Collection of Guns. 82, 83, 84
Partial reproduction of speech in Houston's handwriting. . .125
The Castle on the Hill which Houston dedicated. 136

INTRODUCTION

When Temple Lea Houston was born in the Texas Governors Mansion August 12, 1860, his father, General Sam, was serving as the first governor of Texas. He had twice served the Republic of Texas as president.

Temple inherited many of his father's characteristics and was often called "The Raven's Fledgling."

As a child he would one moment assume the regal manner of some super-important person, often Napoleon, only to later lapse into a silence no one could penetrate.

Both parents passed away before he was seven years of age and he was raised by his sister. He had his mother's talent for the arts, and the ability to read the most technical material and understand the teachings therein. But he also inherited the spirit of adventure with new fields to conquer from his father. These characteristics expressed themselves often in his life but never in conflict, making him a many faceted personality.

His already recognizable talent as an orator won him the presidency of the debating team at the age of nine or ten. He strictly enforced the rules and all forms of order. He went on to speak at the unveiling of the San Jacinto Monument, dedication of the Texas State Capitol Building, and the Castle on the Hill at Northeastern State College, Alva, Oklahoma. He spoke at the Tennessee Centennial, and to a group of ladies on astronomy.

But before he could make a name for himself in oratory, law, and as a politician, a little of the wanderlust inherited from his father had to be worked off. At thirteen he joined a cattle drive to Kansas. He soon began to feel the pinch of hard work, long days, and short nights. He left the drive at trails end and worked his way to the Mississippi River; at fourteen went to work as a night clerk on a river boat. His wit, personality, and ability to imitate the voices of others won him the friendship and respect of the other travelers. One of these passengers obtained a job for him as page in the United States Senate.

Listening to the speeches of the senators he became very

impressed with law. He left his job and returned home and entered Baylor Military Academy.

Here he made top grades, was active in the debating society and was on the editorial staff of a monthly magazine. He graduated at the age of nineteen with honors and then went to work with a judge in Georgetown, again studying law and soon passed the bar examination. However, he was too young, by state law, to practice.

He served as county attorney in Brazoria where he met Laura Cross and fell in love. Their plans to marry had to be postponed when he was appointed district attorney of the Panhandle District, then the wildest and most untamed part of Texas. Temple went ahead to see if he could make a safe and secure home for Laura. When he felt he could, he returned and married his lovely Laura.

A roundabout trip home was their honeymoon. They traveled by train and wagon and had many incidents take place along the way. Life in Mobeetie was a far cry from the luxury Laura had known before but being a strong woman she made the best of what they had.

He was elected senator of Texas to replace Senator A.L. Matlock, where again he was too young to serve. This age discrepancy was waived. He helped pass some remarkable legislation while in office, all the while continually fighting the urge to play practical jokes on senior constituents.

Along the route to success he had many successful times in court battles and a few bad times. In his failures to win, he always fought to the highest court.

Again unable to resist the wanderlust in his blood he joined the "Great Run" when the Cherokee Strip was opened to settlers. As the town of Woodward, Oklahoma, was built, Temple bought a lot and built a house for his family and moved them there. This house was where both Temple and Laura lived out their lives. Temple's wanderlust was abated by the many calls to other places to defend someone charged with a crime.

Temple took an active part in the making of a state of the Territory of Oklahoma. He was being approached by many to run for the first governor of the new state. He was willing but time was not on his side.

I

Trial of Minnie Stacey

Temple Lea Houston strolled into the courtroom. Not having a case on the docket for the day due to a previous illness, he chose to listen to the trials that were being held in the courtroom of Woodward, Oklahoma, as they promised some excitement. He reveled in all phases of his frontier life, especially his law practice for which he had become well-known.

Not only as a lawyer, he was also well-known and in much demand as an orator; he studied the techniques of the most famous lawyers and speakers from the beginning of time. He had studied sentence structure until he had made an art of speech. He had studied people until by looking into their faces he could read their reaction to the progress of a trial. He fought hard against the use of his father's name to enhance his career. The drama of the courtroom and the pleasant enchantment of his family life made up his happy and contented life. Excitement was a tonic to him.

Eccentric in dress, he was still considered by the ladies as the most handsome and personable man they ever met and the men he was associated with admired him for his sincerity, wit, and dedication. They trusted him and always enjoyed working with him or against him on a case.

He was over six feet tall, his brown hair flowing in soft curls to his shoulders, his grey eyes at once piercing the heart with fear or sending forth a message of compassion, tenderness, and love. He usually wore a Prince Albert coat, Spanish-styled, bell bottomed trousers, and a black western hat with a silver eagle on the crown. His boots, always well polished, were a size five and his hands were small enough to wear a ladies glove.

1

The first case on the court docket was The Territory of Oklahoma vs. Minnie Stacey, Cause: Running a Bawdy House and Plying her Trade.

Alone and without benefit of legal counsel, Minnie Stacey appeared in court dressed in a neat but faded dress. Something about the case aroused the indignation of Temple Houston. As he sat listening to the proceedings, the presiding judge, John H. Burford, asked the defendant if she had counsel.

"No, sir," she replied.

"Houston," the Judge asked, "would you act as this woman's counsel?"

"I would be happy to," Temple replied, his voice impaired by his recent illness.

"Then we will recess for ten minutes for you to prepare your case."

Temple had never before met Minnie Stacey. But the phase of the case that stirred him to such righteous indignation as to accept the case on such short notice was that the county attorney claimed she had stolen five hundred dollars from his wallet. Temple's thought was that if she was guilty of that, and the facts were plain that she was guilty of plying her trade and running a bawdyhouse, then the esteemed county attorney must have been availing himself of her services. Yet, now he fought her in court, where he was in his element, for supplying the pleasures he sought. This was all that he knew about the case when court re-convened.

The trial was held in Woodward, Oklahoma, Friday, May 25, 1899.

Although his voice was impaired and he spoke in low tones, he was still able to captivate his audience, his jury, and the rest of the court, his senses as sharp as ever.

He was sensitive and shrank from adversities as a weaker man would not have done. He did not feel that physical violence was needed to express his feelings; he used his ability in speech for this. His defense of the fallen woman was prepared on a moment's notice and was a masterpiece of humility, reaching out a hand to the helpless.

2

He addressed the jury in a conversational tone, standing near enough that he could reach out and touch each of them with his hand. He opened his appeal by re-stating the legal question involved and discussing the evidence. He bent even closer to the jury and began his appeal in a clear voice and closed his summation with these words:

"Gentlemen, you heard with what cold cruelty the prosecution referred to the sins of this woman, as if her condition were of her own preference. The evidence has painted you a picture of her life and surroundings. Do you think they were of her own choosing? Do you think she willingly embraced a life so revolting and horrible? Ah, No! Gentlemen, one of our own sex was the author of her ruin, more to blame than she; then let us judge her gently. What could be more pathetic than the spectacle she presents? An immortal soul in ruin—where the star of purity once glittered, shame has set its seal forever; and only a moment ago they reproved her for the depths of which she had sunk, the company she kept, the life she led. Now, what else is left her? Where can she go and her sin not pursue her?

"Gentlemen, the very promises of God are denied her. He said: 'Come unto me all ye that labor and are heavy laden and I will give you rest.' She had indeed labored and is heavy laden, but if at this instant she were to kneel down before us all and confess her Redeemer and beseech his tender mercies, where is the church that would receive her? And even if they accepted her, when she passed the portals to worship and claim her rest, scorn and mockery would greet her and those she met would gather around them their skirts the more closely, to avoid the pollution of her touch. Would you tell me a single employment where she can realize?

"Give us this day our daily bread?" Our sex wrecked her once pure life—her own sex shrink from her as they would the pestilence. Society has reared its relentless walls against her, and only in the friendly shelter of the grave can her betrayed and broken heart ever find the Redeemer's promised rest. They told you of her assumed names, as fleeting as the shadows on the walls, of her sins, her habits, but they never told you of her sor-

3

rows, and who shall tell what her heart, sinful though it may be, now feels.

"When the remembered voices of mother and sisters, whom she must see no more on this earth, fall like music on her erring soul and she prays God that she could only return, and must not—no, not in this life, for the seducer has destroyed the soul. You know the story of the prodigal son, but he was a son. He was one of us, like her destroyer; but for the prodigal daughter there is no return. Were she with her wasted form and bleeding feet, to drag herself back to home, she, the fallen and the lost, what would be her welcome? Oh, consider this when you come to decide her guilt; for she is before us, and we must judge her. They sneer and scoff at her. One should respect her grief, and I tell you, there reigns over her penitent and chastened spirit of desolation now that none, no, none, but the searcher of all hearts can ever know.

"None of us are utterly evil, and I remember that when the Saffron Scourge swept over the city of Memphis in 1878, a courtesan there opened wide the doors of her gilded palace of sin to admit the sufferers; and when the scythe of the reaper swung fast and pitiless she was angelic in her ministering. Death called her in the midst of her mercies and she went to join those she tried to save. She, like those the Lord forgave, was a sinner, and yet I believe that in the day of reckoning her judgment will be lighter than those who persecute and seek to drive off the earth such poor unfortunates as she whom you are to judge.

"They wish to fine this woman and make her leave. They wish to wring from the wages of her shame the price of this meditated injustice; to take from her the little money she might have: and God knows, Gentlemen, it came hard enough. The old Jewish law told you that the price of a dog nor the hire of such as she should not come within the house of the Lord, and I say unto you that our justice fitly symbolized by a woman's form, does not ask at your hands the pitiful privilege of being left alone.

"The Master while on earth, while he spoke in wrath and rebuke to the kings and rulers, never reproached one of these. One He forgave, another he acquitted. You remember both,

4

and now looking upon this friendless outcast if any of us can say unto her, 'I am holier than thou' in the respect with which she is charged with sinning, who is he? The Jews who brought the woman before the Savior have been held up to the execration of the world for two thousand years. I always respect them. A man who will yield to the reproaches of his conscience as they did has the elements of good in him, but the modern hypocrite has no such compunctions. If the prosecutors of this woman whom you are trying had but brought her before the Savior they would have accepted his challenge and each one gathered a rock and stoned her in the twinkling of an eye.

"No, Gentlemen, do as your Master did twice under the very circumstances that surround you. Tell her to go in peace."

The jury acquitted her as soon as they could reach their room.

There was one newspaper article that stated that she was caught again plying her trade in Texas and Oklahoma Panhandles on several occasions after that; however, the dates given are supposedly taken from court records dated from 1891 until 1898 and this trial was not until 1899. As far as other records show, she was never heard from again after this trial. Some say she moved to another state and changed her life, married, and became a well-respected woman. Possibly Temple's plea to the jury was also a plea to her that she listened well to. When Temple passed away there was a wreath of flowers at his funeral bearing her name.

References

Plains Indian and Historical Museum, Woodward, Oklahoma; Houston Collection.
Court Records, Woodward, Oklahoma.
Amarillo Glove News, June 4, 1972; Temple Houston's Great Oratory Became Legendary, by George Turner.

BIRTHPLACE of Temple Lea Houston, Texas Governor's Mansion in 1866. —*Courtesy Austin-Travis County Collection, Austin, Library.*

6

II

Childhood of Temple Lea Houston

Lawyers and orators still study his techniques and try to emulate the success of Temple Lea Houston. He earned the respect of his legal opponents in the courtroom as well as his clients. Born to fame and glory, he gleaned his success through his own merits and became renowned as an orator at the early age of nineteen because of his taste of knowledge, his capable and often voltairean use of the English language, and his theatrical presentation of a speech; but he never drew on his fathers' fame to further his own career.

Temple Lea Houston, the youngest son of General Sam and Margaret Lea Houston, was the first child born in the Texas Governor's mansion on August 12, 1860 while his father was serving as the first governor of Texas. General Sam had also twice been president of the Republic of Texas. Because of the many characteristics of his father that he inherited, Temple was often called 'The Raven's Fledgling.'

When Temple was born, General Sam, having fought many real and political battles, felt he was now entitled to a period of tranquility to enjoy this youngest son. He was sixty-seven years of age and his other children had somehow grown away from him during his many absences from home. This dream was not to be, because of the civil strife in the United States. Many Texans were wanting secession and others were wanting to remain with the Union, as did General Sam. He had one more bitter battle to fight. He was ousted from his position as governor, being overruled by a majority vote to secede from the Union. Older than his years, ill from too much strife, and embittered to see his long fight for statehood being thrown away, General Sam lived only three more years.

Sired by a man who had struggled long and hard for his country and Texas, sacrificing personal riches, taking pride and fervent pleasure in the building of this young and growing country, Temple had a great heritage to live up to. Many things were expected of him that were not called for in a boy of ordinary birth. He met the challenge.

Temple was only one year old when his father moved from the governors' mansion to their home in Independence. A slave owner himself, General Sam still felt that remaining with the Union was the only way to preserve it. The pressure and personal thrust at his pride were too much for the tired old man, and he began to age fast. They moved from Independence to Huntsville and were living in the Steamboat House when he died. Temple was not quite three years old.

Margaret Lea Houston had been born and raised as a genteel Southern belle but withstood the hardships and disappointments of her husband's career with dignity. Now widowed, Mrs. Houston moved with her children from Huntsville back to Independence and purchased a home nearer to town. She had two lively young sons under the age of nine, Temple and William. She needed to be near her older daughter, Nancy, now Mrs. J.C.S. Morrow.

Mrs. Houston often wrote her eldest son, Sam Jr., who was serving in the Confederate Army, how much she needed him to help raise these two boys who were often a source of amusement as well as chagrin to the already saddened mother.

As a lad, Temple often played with the saddle, girding, and sword of General Santa Anna whom his father had defeated in battle at San Jacinto. He was a happy child, occasionally assuming a superabundance of importance in a most regal manner, the next moment shrinking into a silence no one could penetrate, alone with his dreams and thoughts. Often in his play, he would pin back the bottom of his coat and assume the stance of Napoleon, his idol in history.

The adventurous spirit that was the guideline of his father

began to show up early in his life. Much of the personal charm and magic that make public idols of men was born in Temple as it had been in his father. He was torn between the lust for adventure, the wild, untamed frontier, and the chance of meeting the most prominent men as well as the most despicable, and their own form of life, and the liking of art, reading and study of the classics and Bible that he inherited from his mother. He solved this dilemma when he often played at war by drawing sketches of battles, with the South always the victor. He always took the sketches to his mother for approval. One instance, there were many more dead Yankee soldiers than usual, and this bothered Mrs. Houston. Was her young son becoming a bloodthirsty warrior? Was he thinking too much of war? Or was it simply his art that he was proud of and his subject was chosen because it was the main topic of all conversations of the time? In an effort to change the subjects of his art without discouraging the art itself, she explained to the small boy that these men were all loved by someone back home; maybe even had a small boy like himself. "They all had souls and someone to love," she continued.

"Yes, I know," he said with a studied frown on his small brow, "they all died Christians."

When the war was over and soldiers began to return home, one troop was passing through Independence and it was necessary that it pass in front of the Houston home. Young Temple ran into the street, waving a Confederate sword someone had given him, and shouting, "If you are Yankees, Halt! You can go no further. But if you are Rebels, you may pass."

Delighted with this kind of reception from a five-year-old boy the soldiers cheered him for as long as they were within sight.

Mrs. Houston passed away two years later. Temple, not quite seven, was left in the care of his sister, Mrs. Margaret Williams, and her husband, W.L. Williams. Along with her brothers, Mrs. Williams also inherited old Aunt Liza, a former slave of Mrs. Houston. Liza had rocked and nursed each of the Houston children. She refused to leave the Houstons when the war was over and she was freed, because she knew no other home or family. Temple delighted in repeatedly hearing the story of how Liza came to be a part of the family. It is an interesting story and tells much of the upbringing of Margaret Lea Houston.

As a small child, Liza and several other negro children were playing near a bridge when a man drove by in a covered wagon, stopped, and talked with the children. He asked if they wanted to ride a little way. Delighted, the children scampered to get in the back of the wagon in shade of the canvas. They rode for some time, not realizing the time because of their play and laughter. The next thing they knew they were on the auction block in New Orleans. Temple Lea bought little Liza and took her home. He called his family together and lined them up and told the little girl to choose the one she wanted to be her mistress. Never faced with a decision before, the child was frightened. Finally after looking them over carefully, she decided on Miss Margaret. For the rest of her life she claimed this to be her first, her best, and most rewarding decision. When Margaret grew up and married Sam Houston, Liza naturally went along and stayed with some of the family until her death. She was buried in the family plot at Independence along with Margaret Houston and her mother.

Except for occasional periods of depression, Temple was happy with his sister. However, he was a kindred spirit of both his father and mother. He had his mother's talent for art, and her ability to read even the most technical material and absorb the teachings therein; but he also had his father's spirit of the wanderlust, new fields to conquer, a restless spirit much akin to the earlier pioneers. He loved the frontier and this began to possess his thoughts more and more as he grew older.

His already recognizable talent as an orator, his readiness to be on top of the matter was possibly one of the reasons he was elected president of the debating team when he was nine or ten years of age. Under his leadership, rules and regulations along with all forms of order were strictly enforced.

One incident his brother, William, delighted in telling typifies his sincerity and ability as a leader. While Temple was in the chair one night, one of the town characters strolled in to listen to one of the debates. He proceeded to make himself comfortable by stretching out full length on one of the benches. Temple banged the gavel and thundered, "Mr. A., you will please assume a proper attitude."

Mr. A. promptly complied and the laughter was loud and general until Temple again used the gavel and demanded order. Order was restored and the debates continued without further incident.

When he was thirteen, his kindred spirit with his father won out and he mounted his pony and rode north, away from the security of his sister's home, to join a cattle drive to Kansas. He was tall and well-built for his age and was generally accepted by the other trail hands as a man, he did his share of the work without complaint. He, like his father, wanted to see, to be a part of the ever expanding frontier. Fearing that he would lose this opportunity, he made his choice at an early age.

He soon began to realize that instead of constant fascination, the life of a cowhand, wandering to new places with the cattle drive, meant long, hot, dusty days in the saddle and short nights sleeping on the cold, hard ground. Yet he never complained, nor was he ready to return to the comfort of his sister's home when the drive was over.

It was during his tenure as a cowboy that he came into possession of his first gun and developed his skill as a marksman. He also learned to respect the gun and consider it a weapon for law and order and not as a proud possession to be used maliciously against those who did not please him.

He left the drive in Kansas and worked his way to the Mississippi River where, at fourteen, he was hired as a night clerk on a river boat. It was here he began, unconsciously, his theatrical training that was to bring such impact on others later in life. He would mimic the voices and mannerisms of the passengers to the delight of all. With his wonderful ability to imitate these manners and habits of men he had met only once, he was a constant source of entertainment to the travelers of the Mississippi. The men began to seek his companionship because he was a likeable young man who demanded respect. Here too,

TEMPLE LEA HOUSTON, age 12. —*Courtesy of Mrs. Mary Hender-son, reproduced by Austin Camera Shop, Abilene, Texas.*

he learned many things that a boy of his age should have been sheltered from. He took these bits of knowledge of the world, and the respect of his older companions in his stride, and continued to do his job well.

On one of these trips he chanced to meet an old friend of his father who was serving as United States Senator. In checking back on the records, the only man that could have filled this category was James W. Flanagan. He served in the House of Representatives at the same time Sam Houston was serving as United States Senator from Texas. During Houston's battle to keep Texas from seceding from the Union, Flanagan was one of his strongest and most loyal supporters. Although Sam Houston left politics in 1861 and died in 1863, Flanagan was active in politics until 1875, a year after he gave Temple a chance to experience a new and exciting life. He got him a job as page in the United States Senate.

In doing so it redirected Temple's life into the field of law and oratory. He listened closely to the speeches, marveling at the composure, the dignity, and the respect that these men took as a matter of everyday life. He began to study law. Sargent Prentiss, who long presided in the Senate, became one of his idols. He also studied the speeches for what they contained and how they were delivered, and soon was convinced that he, too, could be a great speaker if he had more education.

He made his decision, left his job, and returned home to enter school again.

References

Amarillo *Sunday News Globe*, June 4, 1972, "Great Orator Became Legend" by George Turner.

"The Brilliant Eccentric, Temple Houston," by Seiginora Russell Laune, published *Strum's Oklahoma Magazine*, April, 1911.

Personal interview with Mrs. Mary Henderson, San Antonio, Texas, September, 1972.

TEMPLE LEA HOUSTON, Cadet at Baylor Military Academy.
—*Courtesy of Mrs. Mary Henderson, reproduced by Austin Camera Shop, Abilene, Texas.*

III

College, Bar Examination

Upon his return home, he spoke seriously to his brother-in-law and guardian, J.C.S. Morrow, about his desires. Morrow was so pleased that he immediately took him to Baylor Military Academy, a part of Southwestern University, then located in Independence, and enrolled him. Temple was now seventeen years old and already a tall, handsome young man. He was probably the last of the first-year students to obtain the rank of lieutenant. As the academy grew, only second and third year students made the rank. This rank was earned by achievement in the ranks and in scholastic marks.

While at the academy he served on the editorial staff of "The Texas Collegian," a monthly magazine published jointly by the Austin Library and Calliopean Debating Societies. Temple was an active member of the Calliopean, attending regular meetings and actively debating. He also served as private secretary to the military staff of State A & M College, then under the command of Capt. George T. Olmsted, Jr.

On one occasion, when the Calliopeans debated the Austin Library Society on November 23, 1878, on the question, "Resolved, That the United States has passed the Zenith of its Glory," Houston chose to speak in the negative. When the two societies locked horns a month later on the question, "Resolved, That Ambition Has Exerted a Greater Influence in Controlling the Action of Mankind than his Superstitution," Temple took the affirmative. No record could be found as to the outcome of either debate. However, these were two subjects that his father before him had fought so gallantly for; now, like father—like son, Temple was taking the same stand his father had. At this point, "Old Sam" would have burst with pride in the accomplishments of this young son he had wanted so badly to know and grow with, something he had been denied with his other children because of the demands of his career.

Temple graduated with honors from Baylor Military Academy when he was nineteen, with a Bachelor of Philosophy degree, and joined the office of Judge Duncan G. Smith of Georgetown, where he again studied law. He passed the bar examination quickly but was too young, according to the state laws, to practice law. Among those graduating with Temple were several who also became prominent in various fields. Of the graduating class of ten young men, there was Sam Houston Dixon, Texas historian; Abner G. Lipscomb, state senator from Waller County; and Dr. Charles H. Wedemeyer, prominent educator.

During his studies at the academy, his spirit of revelry was not dead but sufficiently under control that he was never called before the dean for misconduct. He not only had a capacity for hard work, but possessed what we now term as a photographic memory. Once he had studied or read his subject, it was remembered with astounding accuracy.

Upon his graduation, Dr. Wm. C. Crane, then president of Baylor University, remarked that as many schools as he had conducted, he had never met a boy with a brighter mind, with quicker perception, and with a mental grasp that was almost measureless. For a boy, he thinks like a mature man, Dr. Crane added.

Young Temple was selected to give the dedication address for the San Jacinto Monument. This speech was given April 21, 1880, when he was only nineteen years old and very inexperienced in the field of public oratory. Yet it also coincided closely with his graduation from the military academy and his association with Judge Smith. It is reasonable to assume that this choice was made partly because he was the youngest son of the hero of San Jacinto, partly because he had already shown great aptitude for eloquently holding the attention of an audience, and partly because of his love and knowledge of history.

The speech was a tribute to the memory of the men who

fought for the independence of Texas and their families, to those who followed to build and inhabit the state; and an emotional plea for the continuance of such great loyalty and dedication.

Trained and ready for a career, Temple Houston was too young to practice law. Several of his friends and colleagues began to make contacts and appeals in his behalf and an exemption from the age law, which was that he must be twenty-one years of age, was obtained for him. He became the youngest practicing attorney in Texas when he opened offices in Brazoria in partnership with a Mr. Vernon.

His law practice paid only a pittance and many of his clients paid him only with a handshake. He did not press for cash payments because most of his clients ranked among the very poor. It was during that period that friendship meant helping out in time of need even if that help was in the realm of the man's livelihood. For a time, Temple took over a local newspaper. Brazoria was the hub of commerce at the time and a good place for a lawyer; but there were already many lawyers there, men with more age and experience and although he was friendly and likeable and soon became well-known, it was still difficult to make a living.

In 1881, the office of county attorney was vacated by the resignation of J.H. Norris when he accepted the appointment of county judge. Temple Houston, not yet twenty-two years of age, was appointed to succeed him. Temple was even now a striking looking person. He was tall, slender, well-built, with brown, curly hair, flashing grey eyes, and a ready smile. He was a practical joker but this was never objectionable because it was well-known that he could take it as well as dish it out. He made friends quickly and easily. Like his father, he took the law and the love of his country very seriously and would allow no deviation or skullduggery.

Temple held this position from the date of his appointment in 1881 until December 23, 1882, when a better and more exciting offer came his way.

References

Interview with Mary Henderson, San Antonio, Texas, and reviewing papers and documents in her possession. September 1972.

Seigniora Russell Laune, "The Brilliant Eccentric Temple Houston," *Strum's Oklahoma Magazine,* April, 1911.

Panhandle *Press Box*, "Temple Houston," by Bob Wright, October 29, 1968.

IV

Romance and Marriage

One night at a dance held in Brazoria, he chanced to look across the room and saw Miss Laura Cross. Their eyes met and immediately both felt the cross-current of an overcharged heart. Temple did not dance and Laura was one of the belles of the ball, beautiful, graceful and one of the best dancers there. This temporarily presented a problem. Not one to let minor things impair his quest, Temple headed straight toward the beautiful young lady. His natural good looks and courteous manner put him in good standing immediately.

Temple bowed low, held out his hand to the beautiful girl and as she placed her delicate hand in his he kissed it gently and said, "My name is Temple Lea Houston."

"I am Laura Cross and I am very happy to make your acquaintance, Mr. Houston."

"Miss Cross, you are not only the most beautiful lady here but you dance so gracefully I only regret that I cannot dance too. However, I would be pleased to know you better. Would you join me in a glass of punch?"

"Yes, thank you."

This was the beginning of a beautiful courtship, a happy and fulfilled marriage, and a life of love for both Temple and Laura. The courtship had not lasted long when they decided that marriage was the thing for them. He succeeded in winning over her family and plans for the wedding were begun.

Laura Cross was truly an aristocrat, having been born and raised on a plantation in Louisiana, with the finest education that could be obtained through governesses and finishing schools. The arts of being a lady were quite natural to her;

however, she waived the time-honored lengthy courtship and chose to marry him very soon.

Before the wedding plans could be completed, however, Governor O.M. Roberts, an archenemy in politics of Sam Houston, asked Temple if he would accept the post of district attorney in the Panhandle District. This could be a ruse to get Temple on his side politically or to get him out of harm's way during the next election. Only those involved at the time would know.

This meant a change in wedding plans and a disruption of his life because the Panhandle District was composed of ten organized counties and forty-four unorganized counties and was wild and untamed. It was not a welcome place to take a bride of Laura's upbringing. The outermost part of the frontier, the excitement of such a place was tempting to his adventurous spirit; but he did not think it a place to take his bride, the woman he had chosen to share the rest of his life with. He was given little time to ponder his decision. The previous district attorney had resigned because of his fear of constant threat of the desperadoes and Indians of the region.

Temple felt that he must go first and find a suitable place to live before taking Laura, if she consented to go at all. He wanted desperately to accept the assignment but he could not help but wonder if such a beautiful and educated lady would give up her accustomed comforts for this wild and untamed new home.

"What do you think of my accepting the appointment?" he asked his betrothed.

Laura already knew him to be adventurous, ambitious, and preferring the frontier to the staid social life of the southern more settled part of Texas. Perhaps this was the part of his charm that she loved most.

"I saw him all the way across the room, and I think he saw me" she had once said. "I guess it was love at first sight all right, for we were both goners. And I began to feel the excitement he got from life and to realize how he felt. I loved him and all I wanted was to be near him."

This new opportunity was so completely unexpected that

Temple feared she might not want to go with him. He explained his impression of what he thought life would be like there, trying very hard not to let his excitement of the chance embellish the facts and paint an untrue picture. He wanted her to know exactly what she would be called upon to face.

"Whatever you want to do, wherever you go, I will be beside you."

"I must go first and see if it is safe for you and if there is a place where you can live comfortably and will be safe. Will you wait for me?"

"Yes, any number of years, if necessary."

The question was settled and the assignment was confirmed December 23, 1882.

With Laura's words fresh in his mind and characteristic of his nature, he left immediately for Mobeetie, Wheeler County, Texas, which was to be his home. His mode of travel is not known, but in a research of the possibilities of the time, it is believed that he traveled part of the six hundred miles by train to Wichita Falls and the rest of the way by horseback.

Barely twenty-two years of age, he was going to the wildest part of Texas to match wits and nerve with the lawless Indians, and other more experienced men of the law.

It took some time for him to get his feet on the ground and to prepare what he considered a fit place to bring his bride. During this time, while riding with posses and in friendly turkey-shoots, his prowess with the gun became well-known. There was a story written about a friendly shooting contest between Temple and Billy the Kid.

Bat Masterson, then sheriff at Tascosa, was very impressed with the new district attorney. He was younger than most men of the law. He did not press his authority openly but would drink sociably with anyone as long as they behaved themselves and kept the conversation on an agreeable basis. Since everyone learned soon after his arrival in Tascosa that Temple was a crack shot with his 'Ole Betsy,' they did not desire to tamper with his temper.

Billy the Kid and his gang rode into Tascosa one day, as was their habit from time to time. Usually when the Kid and his bunch came to town, they tore up the town with their pranks and added much to the population of Boot Hill. Masterson was aiming to stop this sort of unreasonable revelry. In a conversation with The Kid he claimed that the new district attorney could outshoot the Kid.

Believing himself to be the best gunslinger of the west and that there was none who could beat him, the Kid readily accepted the challenge from Masterson that the district attorney was the best. Masterson sought out Temple Houston and a match was arranged behind the adobe saloon. A crowd gathered quickly to watch the shoot-out between the two young men noted for their accuracy with a gun, knowing that there was to be no fight or killing. Masterson tossed a plug of Blue Star chewing tobacco into the air, Temple drew with amazing speed and accuracy and shot the star on the tobacco dead center.

"Quien lo haga mejor," (who could do better) asked the Kid, who paid off his bet and walked away without firing a shot. After this the Kid and his bunch walked softly for a few days, then left Tascosa, never to return.

Many stories have been written about early men of the West and their abilities with a gun, but completely omitting the good and kind side of their lives, the problems that drove them to use the gun, their families, their ambitions, and loves. This consequently left the impression that the majority were lawless gunmen, which was untrue. Under the pen of many writers, Temple was said to be a gunman, fast on the draw, and quick to kill. He was fast with a gun, but used it only to his advantage in upholding the law. He was quoted as saying that if people knew you were good with a gun, they were less likely to start any trouble with you. They tended to respect that ability in the times when most all men carried a gun.

He prepared a home for Laura and about a year after leaving Brazoria he returned, and they were married on February 14, 1883, on the Waldeck Plantation for which her stepfather, Mr. Viella, was overseer. This plantation was once owned by Prince Waldeck, cousin of Queen Victoria. It was then owned by Eastern investors and managed by Mr. Viella.

The bride and groom's honeymoon trip was a circuitious

route back to Mobeetie. Enroute they visited friends and relatives. Their first stop was Galveston where they spent the day on the old Tremont place. The Tremonts were friends of the family and arranged a second wedding for the couple. Since there was no priest in Brazoria, and Laura was a devout Catholic, the second marriage was planned. Laura was married the second time in what was called her "second day" dress.

When the young couple were in Galveston, they visited a friend who owned a jewelry and gift shop. He opened the store, even though it was Sunday, and told the bride to pick out anything her heart desired and it would be his wedding gift to them. Laura, not wanting to chose a gift that was too expensive, chose a decorative blood-red wine bottle. The store owner wrapped the gift and wished them a happy honeymoon and a long and successful life together. Later on the train, Laura unwrapped her gift to examine it more closely. There was a price of $25 on the bottom. The bottle always had a prominent place in their home and is now in the possession of their youngest child, Mary.

On to Houston, they stayed a week at the old capitol and then took the train to Wichita Falls. Everything went smoothly enough until they took a hack and headed westward toward their new home. Their only companion on this part of the trip was Laura's negro servant, old Meliss. They forded icy streams and camped in scantily sheltered places at night.

Late one evening, they saw the curling of smoke of an Indian camp on the opposite bank of the river. They unhitched the horses and went down the side of the draw below and had a cold supper. When the horses had rested a bit they went on.

"I drove while Mr. Houston and Meliss walked," Laura wrote later to a friend, "leading the horses to make as little noise as possible. We had lost the dim trail we had been following and lost some time while trying to find it again. About 2:00 a.m. we made camp to rest a little. At dawn, we were wakened by the sound of a cowbell. We found we had camped near some traders."

The next night, they found an abandoned log hut for shelter.

There were other hazards they encountered. Once, as they

were crossing a stream, the breast yoke broke. Forced to abandon the hack, Temple carried his bride to dry land.

"Would you be afraid to wait here while I go for help?"

"No."

"Then I had best get started."

Laura watched him walk away with many misgivings, would he find help; if so, would he be able to find his way back? All of this part of Texas had a sameness of terrain, was scantily populated, and no outstanding landmarks. Never one to show fear, she shrugged these thoughts off while she and Meliss made themselves as comfortable against the bitter wind as possible. They sat and waited, listening to the howling of the hungry coyotes from about 9:00 a.m. until about three in the afternoon. Still her serenity was not ruffled. Yes, Laura, if any woman ever was, was fitted for the frontier life; yet she was only sixteen years of age.

Temple might well have wandered aimlessly for quite some time in this sparsely-settled untamed country. The wind was bitter cold. Snow lay heavily in the places that the wind had not touched and had not blown away. Coming over a rise in the ground he saw a cowboy mount his horse and ride away from a snow covered mound. It turned out to be a little-used dugout line camp. Several cowboys had taken refuge from the snow, and the one who rode away just pointed out the spot for Temple. Several cowboys remained at the dugout and rode back with Temple to the wreckage of the hack. Soon the honeymoon couple were on their way again.

After the many hardships they had to bear, Laura was hardly prepared for Mobeetie, a town of few frame buildings, sod shanties, and some houses made of cans.

References

Houston Scrapbook, Houston Public Library, Houston, Texas.

Houston Post, April 2, 1936, "Temple Houston and Laura Cross, Lived Romance That Many Today Might Envy," by Melva V. Newton.

Personal interview with Mrs. Mary Henderson, San Antonio, Texas, October 28, 29, 1973.

Harper Bros., New York, "An Informal History of Texas" Chapter on Mobeetie by Frank X. Tolbert, published 1961.

V

Home in Mobeetie

When they moved to Mobeetie, Temple purchased a lot for their home, which was the south half of Section 86, Block 17. It was sold with no water and no fence but with bunch and mesquite grass, and was good for raising corn and oats, millet or other cereal or vegetable products, containing three hundred and twenty acres. The house they built has not been described in any of the material found and my main source of information, Mrs. Henderson, never saw the house. However it was probably a small frame or adobe house and about the only one at that time that had a wood floor. Temple always tried to provide the best for his "Valentine."

While they lived in Mobeetie, Temple Jr. and Louise were born. Louise died during an epidemic of cholera infantum at the age of four and is at rest in some unmarked grave near Mobeetie.

Laura had never cooked a meal nor ironed a dress but this was only an added challenge to the excitement of her new life in the open land and with her love, her husband, who was within himself an exciting man. He continued to be courteous to a fault, to honor and place her on a pedestal of love.

The Houstons did not go out much; their life together was happy in the quiet solitude of their home. However, whenever there was a dance at nearby Fort Elliott, Temple delighted in taking his bride and showing her off, even though he still could not dance. His eyes would light up with love and admiration as he watched her glide across the floor with her many admiring partners. Otherwise, Mrs. Houston lived the quiet life of a small town lawyer's wife, giving her time and energy solely to her

MRS. LAURA CROSS HOUSTON, wife of Temple Lea Houston shown in her "Second-Day Dress." —*Photo courtesy of Sam Houston Museum, Huntsville, Texas. Reproduced by Revelle Studio, Huntsville.*

family. Temple reciprocated in kind; his love for his family was one of his strongest assets.

Speaking of their life in Mobeetie, Mrs. Houston often said, "Many times I have seen a cowboy riding through the streets of Mobeetie shooting a pistol with one hand and taking a drink of whiskey from his bottle with the other. Sometimes they would ride up and down the streets of the town by twos shooting and yelling as loud as they could. But they were harmless and did not mean to give trouble."

She never complained of the hardships she had to endure nor the quality of the house she had to live in. In fact, she bore a lot of the adventurous characteristics of her husband, but they were delicately hidden beneath her charm and beauty.

It was in Mobeetie that Temple began to make a name for himself. The jumbo district was not without law, but the scant coverage of so large an area gave ample time to escape for the would-be outlaw. In matching wits with more experienced lawyers, judges, and ranchers who had pulled their way up by their boot straps under their own brand of law against outlaws and Indians, he was in a realm of activity that brought out his wild and dramatic instincts.

Temple often ignored adults to spend many hours with his and other children, teasing and playing with them. He spent many other hours reading the classics and the Bible, and after reading a passage once, quoting from memory, he quite often pulled from this fantastic memory passages that strengthened a speech or a courtroom plea.

Blessed with this brilliant mind and quick wit, he became a dedicated lawyer and orator. A man unequaled in his time or since, he is a man who now belongs to history. But he does not belong to the public of today to the extent that they can take only a small part of what he was and blow it up into a fabricated accumulation of half truths, leaving the impression that he was often on the wrong side of the law or that he was a figment of the imagination that people held because he had once done them a good turn. Many authors have taken great liberties with small fragments of information and embellished it to make a

27

quick selling short article and in doing this some of the truths of this man have been obscured.

Most of the people in the Panhandle District considered him eccentric, for in comparison to their common, serviceable and non-descript attire, his was flambouyant even to the black sombrero with a silver eagle on the crown, frock tail coat, and small high heel, well polished boots. He also carried a pearl handled six-shooter which he called 'Old Betsy.' Eccentric in dress though he was, the people loved him, especially the children who turned to him when a question came up that needed a quick answer. He never turned a deaf ear to a child.

He was once described as "modest as a blushing maiden, courageous as a knight, poetic as a lover of the time of the troubadours." His natural flambouyance was unequaled. His courtesy to the ladies was proverbial and he had a passionate fondness for all that was beautiful. He loved practical jokes and could pull them off with clever nonchalance, or take the brunt of one with equal calm.

He was a child of nature and loved the frontier. He would rather live in a shanty on the bleak prairie within sight of the Indians than to live in a palace and enjoy the society of lords and ladies.

He was never accused of vanity; in fact, he was so devoid of such luxury that he never had his picture taken willingly. There was never a family portrait made, as most families did in that time, because he did not want to be in it.

Long dissertations on his many courtroom appearances would be boring to the reader, but because of his flare for the dramatic whenever it was known that Temple Houston would be in the courtroom, crowds thronged to hear him speak and were entranced at his ability to, at will, quote from memory the Bible or the classics. They knew that they would either hear a serious plea for his clients or that he would delve into sarcasm against his legal opponent, never, however, to the extent that he ever lost a friend from it. Some of his most noted speeches will be included in a separate section, along with the circumstances that put him in this position, while the shorter ones will be a part of the text of the first part. When you know the man, the flare for dictum, the drama involved, you will want to read these speeches as he would have spoken them.

On one of Houston's trips on court business to Amarillo he visited with Judge J.D. Hamlin after court adjourned. Soon both were well in their cups and in a jovial and talkative mood.

"Hamlin," Houston said, "I think you would be a good candidate for the House of Representatives and I intend to nominate you at the next convention."

"Ah, No! Houston, I have too much work to do here."

Further conversation and Temple's persuasive manner soon had the two men planning the campaign in every detail, with a drink or two between each idea. Temple sat down and wrote a number of letters to old-time friends of his in various counties of the Panhandle, urging them to support his warm and personal friend, Judge J.D. Hamlin.

After Temple left for home and the Judge had recovered from his spree, he realized that it would be a fool thing for him. However, by this time several counties such as Potter and Armstrong and six others were already pledged to support him.

At the convention Judge Hamlin asked his friend Judge Browning to announce that Hamlin wished his name taken from consideration as a candidate.

References

West Texas Historical Assn. Yearbook, Vols. 6-10, 1930-34, June, 1930, Pages 12 and 13, Old Mobeetie, The Capital of the Panhandle, by L.F. Sheaffy.
Strum's Oklahoma Magazine, Vol. 12, No. 2, Pages 20-23, April 1911, The Brilliant, Eccentric Temple Houston, by Seigniora Russell Laune.
The Flambouyant Judge, James D. Hamlin; as told to J. Evetts Haley and Wm. Curry Holden, published by Palo Duro Press, 1972 Canyon, Texas. Copyright, Palo Duro Press.

VI

Texas Senator From The Panhandle

Senator A.L. Matlock of the 56th (Jumbo) District of Texas resigned and at the general election November 4, 1884, Temple Houston was elected senator. This district was comprised of an area larger than the state of New York. Again, he was two years younger than the state required age for the position, and again, due to lack of qualified men from the area who were willing to serve, this age discrepancy was waived. It seemed that he was always two years ahead of himself as well as the rest of Texas. He had already proven himself as a brilliant lawyer and was respected throughout the state. He was following in his father's footsteps and again with due respect to the dignity of his position, as he did when he was in college, he held his wild streak under control. It must have been difficult, with so many opportunities offering themselves for his particular brand of practical jokes and his caustic remarks, for him to keep himself in check and not carry out these jokes. But he did respect the dignity of the men and the offices they held, and was never known to pull a joke on them. Even his speeches were often toned down so that none of his senior constituents would feel the prick of what could often be a caustic remark aimed at the human frailties of others. He dropped his theatricalism except when he deemed it necessary to make a point; then he delved into his most proverbial poetic repertoire to enhance his cause.

He served in the regular session of the 19th Legislature from January 13 to March 31, 1885; the 20th Legislature from January 15 to April 4, 1887 and a special session from April 16 to May 15, 1888. During the time he took an active interest in the Alamo Church property, supporting the resolution that it be turned over to the City of San Antonio. He supported the resolution that the chaplain of the Senate officiate at the ceremony laying the cornerstone of the new state capitol building. Later he was chosen to give the dedication speech for this landmark.

He served on many committees preparing resolutions to be presented to the Senate. He was a patriotic and religious man but was not active in any church until in his later days when he embraced the Catholic faith, which was the lifelong faith of his wife, Laura.

He was the author of many bills, chief of which provided pensions for children of Texas martyrs. Framed and hanging within the walls of the Alamo is a copy of the Alamo Purchase Bill with the powerful appeal to the old building.

He served on committees in connection with the treasury, the Panhandle grasslands, law enforcement, and the school systems of Texas.

While serving as a Senator, he attended a political meeting to nominate a candidate for the United States Senate. The meeting began slowly with no one showing the promise of an idea. Temple took the reins. This was one of his unprepared and unrehearsed speeches but in the nomination of Sam Bell Moxey for re-election, Temple brought the minds and hearts of all present back to the reality of their purpose, "to serve the people to the best of their ability and in the best interests of the people."

He ruined his political prospects by a vicious attack on the Court of Appeals because that body failed to rule as he felt it should. This probably had some connection with the trial of the Vernon minister where the Court of Appeals upheld the original verdict of guilty. He was already disillusioned by the "bigotry and strategy" used in obtaining the passage of some bills that were not adequate or were flagrant insults to the State of Texas. Fearlessly, he denounced the Court of Appeals, knowing it would affect his political future. But, like his father, he considered the rights of others, the future of Texas, and his own ideals of integrity above that of furthering his own political future or in personal monetary gain.

31

After leaving the Senate, he moved from Mobeetie to Canadian where he lived for several years and practiced law as a defense attorney. In Canadian, two more children were born to Temple and Laura, Sam III and Laura. Laura only lived six months and was buried like her sister on the plains of Texas.

H.E. Hoover, attorney in Canadian, who was intimately associated with Houston once wrote: "While Napoleon was his ideal of true greatness, he nevertheless did not aspire to riches, honor or public admiration. It is true that his manner of dress always attracted public ridicule rather than admiration, yet his peculiarity of dress was the result of his eccentric character rather than a desire to attract public notice. In fact his manner of dress, as well as his public and private life, each was the result of his own idea of what they should be without the least regard as to what the public might say or think, and certainly without intention to draw attention to himself to further his career."

Near the end of his term as Senator, the Santa Fe Railroad was building across the Indian Territory of Oklahoma and the plains of Texas. Temple was retained to obtain the right of way and continued as their attorney for the area until his death.

With his natural fluency and his popularity with the people he came in contact with, he could have amassed a fortune and had a political career. However, he ruined his political future in Texas by speaking frankly against the decision of the Court of Appeals rather than let his friends down. This outburst was to affect many other decisions in his life later on. Money meant very little to him. He did not aspire to fame at the cost of his honesty and integrity which he felt he would sacrifice if he continued his political career. Houston ignored the lobbying he hated so much. His only desire was to live with the growth of the frontier and his family. This was an admirable quality except that at his death it left his family almost penniless. There was the treasure of expensive gifts to his wife, but these Laura could not sell; they were too much a part of their love.

For natural Ciceronian speech, he had few equals and no superiors. In the practice of law he was an eccentric, not always agreeing with the court's decision, but his faith in law and order as such never waivered, only his personal judgment of certain men. When he believed an injustice was meted out by the courts, his patience was stretched to the limits of his endurance. He outwardly spoke his displeasure and either let it remain at that or appealed to higher courts. If he believed a man innocent, he would defend him to the best of his ability and a fee was the last thing he thought of.

Once when he was especially angry by the verdict against his client, he left the courtroom and was heard to mutter, "If I started to hell with a load of ice to sell, the damn place would freeze over before I got there."

References

Texas Congressional Records, 1884 through 1888, Texas State Capitol, Austin, Texas.
Amarillo Sunday News-Globe, June 4, 1972 Page 1-D, "Temple Houston's Great Oratory Became Legendary," by George Turner.

VII

Court Trials

While living in Canadian, his reputation had grown so extensively that he was called upon to defend many who were at odds with the law. This took him to various parts of Texas, New Mexico, Oklahoma, and Kansas. None of these cases were given in detail, or the location of the trial, so no court records were available. His cases were so many and so exciting that most writers only listed the interesting facts and did not give the location of the trial. However, the little known bits of information do give some insight as to the true character of Temple Lea Houston.

He lived every day to the fullest, grasping every opportunity to help his friends in trouble or even a stranger whenever he felt within his heart that he was innocent or was being tried for some other reason than stated in the charges. He lived each day as if it were to be his last.

As an orator he had no counterpart. His vocabulary was extensive, his dictum beautiful. He studied constantly and in reading the classics, Plato was his favorite. Time traveling on the train was not wasted; he either read quietly, absorbing within his fabulous memory every word, or he found an interesting companion. Knowing people was his business.

One of his little-known cases took him to New Mexico on a call for help from a classmate at Baylor Military Academy. This man's son was to be tried for a murder.

There was no delay. Temple headed for New Mexico to assist his friend. He won the case and the boy was freed. However, Temple refused payment or even reimbursement for his travel expenses. His friend was a successful rancher and could have well afforded to pay a good fee. This was one of the reasons that Temple Houston died leaving his family in near poverty.

Later, he was called to Kansas to defend a man charged with selling stolen cattle. This was to go down in the records as the shortest defense in court records.

The town where the trial was held was a shipping center for the cattle driven up from Texas to the railhead. The business men in town had 'cleaned up' on the wages of the cowhands, lonesome from long months with the herd.

Temple was careful to see that the men chosen as jurors were the most prominent business men of the town. As the prosecuting attorney finished with each witness, it was Temple's time to question them.

"No questions," he said with each witness.

When the prosecuting attorney completed his summation, again it was Houston's turn to impress the jury. Rising to his full height, looking very dignified with his solemn expression, his Prince Albert coat and Mexican style trousers, he hooked his thumbs in the pockets of his brocaded vest and faced the jurors, looking each one in the eye. They had, by their expressions, already decided on a verdict of guilty. He took a moment to look at each of them and then began his summation.

"Gentlemen of the jury, it is obvious as I stand here and look at you that each of you are successful at his trade and can be possibly classified as wealthy. This town and your wealth was built solely upon the cattle driven up from the south to be sold here. If you choose to try every man who sells a steer of questionable ownership, I predict that within less than a year this will be a ghost town and your wealth will be like the dust of this vast prairie, gone in a puff of wind."

With that he sat down. The jury being duly admonished as to their duties took less than one minute to bring in a verdict of 'not guilty.'

Another trial where he was not so successful was in the defense of a Vernon minister for the murder of his wife. Temple was very bitter with the outcome and tried every appeal available to him only to have the original verdict upheld on each appeal. This case was possibly the bitterest defeat in his career and very probably prompted his outburst against the Texas Court of Criminal Appeals.

Glib and quick with words and saying just what he thought whether in court or not, he once told a presiding judge about the opposing attorney for whom he had taken quite a dislike: "Your Honor, this is the only man I know who can strut while sitting down."

References

Amarillo Globe News, June 4, 1972, "Temple Houston Great Oratory Became Legendary" by George Turner.

Sam Houston Museum, Huntsville, Texas, Files and Records on Temple Lea Houston.

VIII

The Run, New Friends, New Life

Standing on the rear platform of the coach the Santa Fe Railroad had furnished for their officials to observe the run, Temple Houston felt a surge of blood rush through his veins as he viewed the spectacle before him. He had chosen to be an observer rather than a participant in the Great Run when the Cherokee Strip of Oklahoma was opened for settlement, but the excitement of the moment had touched him deeply.

It was September 16, 1893, and the day was hot and sultry. Horses, wagons, surreys, carts, and other conveyances choked the air with the dust they stirred up. Temple, along with other Santa Fe officials, stood on the platform. The wind blew the long brown hair back from his face, revealing grey eyes alight with expectancy, a flush of excitement that was a part of his nature, showing in his face. He watched the horses straining at the bits to get started as if they too felt the stimulus of the event.

Some of these people were beginning life, newly wed with new lives and a new start; some were single men hoping to set up a homestead so they could marry and have a family of their own. Still others were families that had repeatedly moved from one place to another, hoping each time and praying that this was their Shangri-la, their final home, the place they could set down roots. Fear, hope, and dreams rode with the people and Temple felt every mood as he watched their faces.

There were several incidents that can be classified as the reason for Houston's move to Oklahoma. He had always felt that he had been living in the shadow of his famous father and he wanted very desperately to be his own man. Secondly, there

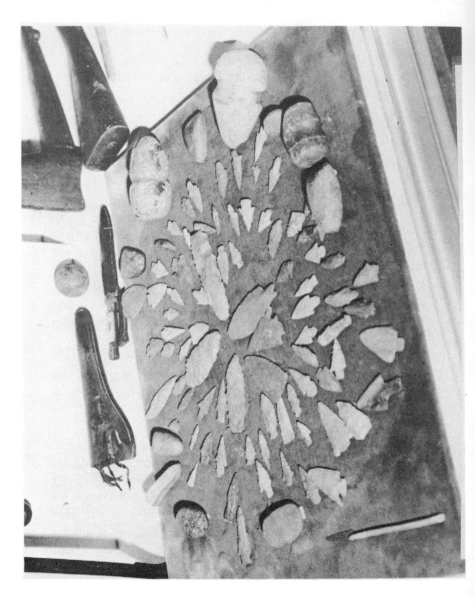

PART of Indian artifacts collection, arrowheads from all tribes, knife, grinding stones, and tomahawks heads.

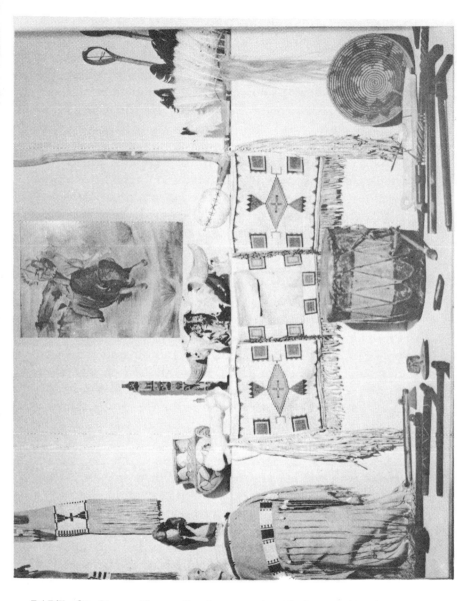

PART of Indian artifacts collection, mostly gifts from Indian friends.
—*Courtesy Sam Houston Museum, Huntsville, Texas.*

was the recent brush with the Texas Court of Criminal Appeals where he spoke freely of his feelings, knowing full well it would go down on record against him. Thirdly, and probably the most prevalent, was the opening of a new frontier where the establishment of law and order was of utmost importance and it offered greater excitement. Temple still felt the call of new frontiers to tame.

Temple left his family in Canadian for almost a year as he set up his practice in Woodward. In the beginning, there were no houses, only shanties and tents, and this was no place for his "Valentine" and their children. When there were available living quarters, he moved them to Woodward where his three youngest children were born: Richard, their youngest son; another daughter who died two weeks after birth; and Mary Lea, the youngest and only girl to survive. Temple and Laura had almost despaired of raising a daughter and when Mary came along, healthy, pretty, vivacious, and very precocious, there was nothing denied her. Her father could not have said "no" to any of his children and this beautiful little girl had him mesmerized, hypnotized, and purely devoted. Even Laura found it difficult to admonish or punish this child, although she took spoiling in her stride as if it was the way she was supposed to be treated. It did, at times, cause problems with her brother and playmates. Her older brother, Sam, was almost as bad as his parents in the spoiling; he was her idol.

Shortly after his arrival in Woodward, he became acquainted with another attorney, Sidney Benton Laune. Their friendship developed into a bond that withstood many a courtroom battle when the men were on opposing teams. Temple was thirty-three years old, a seasoned lawyer that had tasted well the heady wine of success; yet he was modest and unassuming. Laune was fresh out of the University of Michigan Law School.

Laune was elected district attorney on the first ballot, placing him constantly on the opposite sides of legal battles with Houston. Once the sheriff had arrested a man for horse stealing. He was riding the horse at the time, and the sheriff placed him in jail. He languished there for several days because he had no

40

money for a lawyer to defend him. The sheriff, judge, and Laune prevailed upon Temple to defend him.

"I will if I can have a room arranged for a private conversation with the man."

"We will take care of that; you just give him the best advice you can," Laune responded.

A room was set up in a nearby office. Before going into the room for a talk with his client, he looked back at the three county officials and flashed his famous grin.

"You can rest assured, gentlemen, that any advice I give this poor unfortunate fellow will be good advice."

After a reasonable lapse of time the three waiting men entered the office. There sat Temple, comfortably at ease with his feet propped on the table. Across the room was an empty chair and an open window.

"Well, boys," Temple said, "I gave him some good advice."

Rarely was there space at the hitchrack or stables for another buggy, wagon, or horse when Temple Lea Houston was in court. He was always the main character and people were sure of a good show whether it be an eloquent plea with frequent references to the Bible or the classics, or one laced with humor. He could easily call upon his repertoire of wit, sarcasm, and quotations without having prepared them in his speech. Whatever he said usually depended upon the impression the witnesses, the facts, and the opposing counsel had made on the jury. His purpose was solely to defend his client to the best of his ability; if necessary he would play upon their sympathy, or their resistibility. In an argument for his client he would sometimes dart this way and that like a well-trained cutting horse, smoothly keeping the line of thought as far from his besmirched client as possible. He often used ridicule of his opponent to keep this distraction and confusion. Sometimes this was in soft, pious tones, branding him a heartless bounder who was preying on the innocent; and at other times using his most dramatic flare of emotion.

Paul Laune, son of Sidney Laune, recalls in his article about

41

Temple Houston, published in *Oklahoma Today*, a story his father loved to tell. Laune was the prosecutor, Temple the attorney for the defense. Temple, following his usual practice of seeing only the jury and talking only to them, launched into the following story:

"Gentlemen of the jury, last night after pondering the insidious machinations of men and their relentless vengeance and vindictiveness aimed at the poor unfortunates that may have momentarily strayed, I fell finally into a troubled sleep. I dreamed that I had died and it may not cause astonishment to learn that in the dream I went to hell."

Here he drew heavily on Dante, describing the inferno and his meeting with the devil himself.

"He was writhing on his throne, his forked tail curling and entwining itself about his legs. I came closer and asked, 'What possibly can have brought you, Your Satanic Majesty, to such a state of despair?' From his glowing eyes the devil gave me a searing glance. 'Temple' he said, 'I have lost my job. All through the vaults of hell the rumor is flying that I am to be replaced.'

'But who,' I asked, 'could conceivably replace you?'

'Rumor has it,' replied Satan, his voice came rumbling with all the fetid breaths of Hades, 'that I am to be replaced by that arch fiend, Sidney Laune.' "

Paul Laune goes on to say that his father would get so swept away by fond memories of those days and the tumultous and often very funny episodes in the courtroom with his good friend, Temple Houston, that he always forgot to say who won the case.

Often, when not occupied in court or with a client, Sidney Laune and Temple Houston lounged in Laune's office, discussing a topic dear to both, history. Both were well versed on the subject and it became an automatic source of conversation. Temple would lie back on an old leather couch and sketch as they talked. One picture he drew of Napoleon on a page in a ledger book. His admiration for Napoleon was second only to that he held for his father, General Sam. The sketch was drawn quickly and was a remarkable likeness, bi-cornered hat, high collar, and all. Then, characteristic of his insatiable enthusiasm, he raced downstairs to a stationery store, bought a child's watercolor set, and rushed back to put his drawing in color. Sadly, after the death of Sidney Laune, this sketch was not found among his effects. This is one of the many instances where he displayed some of the traits and talents inherited from his mother, Margaret Lea Houston.

Sidney Laune was probably the closest friend of Temple. Certainly they had their professions, their love for history, and a common bond of respect that kept them in close confidence with each other. Their association over the years gave them an insight to the character of the other, and naturally they told their innermost secrets. They knew each other as brothers might. Sidney Laune was quick to say that Temple's prowess with a gun was often misrepresented. Good, yes, but quick to draw on another, never. He said that one could count on one hand, with fingers left over, the number of times he had drawn his gun against another man, and that these included his trouble with both the Jennings family and Joe Jenkins. He stated that his marksmanship was outstanding and Temple strove to keep it such because just the knowledge that he was good with a gun helped him in many instances. Considering that the day in which he lived was the ending of the era of carrying weapons and the beginning of the law and order he strove to uphold, he was one of the first men to encourage gun control laws and to prevent the wearing of sidearms in town.

Like many men of the Old West, Temple was involved in many a stern drama. But in the telling of these incidents the lighter, warmer side of his personality, the part of him that those who knew him, and loved and respected him knew so well, had been sadly neglected.

His wife, Laura, related the stories of the Indians' devotion to her husband. In the early days in Oklahoma, she was often required to entertain Indians as guests until they chose to leave or until her husband came home. These were friends of Temple and they considered his home open to their visits at any time. They almost worshipped her husband and would often come to visit her, six or eight warriors at a time. They would sit in a circle around the wall and talk among themselves and smile at her; she would smile in return and go on about her work. She knew only a little of their language but felt no fear of them. They would never harm the woman who belonged to the man they so admired. She did, of course, take care of her actions so that none of them would feel insulted or unwanted. They were very unpredictable in their behavior pattern, especially when they felt that they had been personally affronted.

When Quanah Parker visited, he would spread a blanket in front of the Houston home and invite them to come out and smoke the peace pipe. Quanah spoke English and did so in her presence. She once stated that she would go through the motions of smoking the pipe but didn't really smoke. If Quanah ever noticed the difference he politely ignored the fact, probably because she belonged to Temple Houston, a man he greatly respected and trusted. Quanah Parker, knowing both Indian and English languages, was not an easy man to fool.

Through Temple Houston's friendship with the Indians, he was able to accumulate some Indian relics that would have otherwise been lost to the public today. Mrs. Houston gave them to the Plains Museum at Woodward and Sam Houston Memorial Museum at Huntsville when he died. Some of these were dresses worn by the women of the tribe, and one especially made for little Mary, as well as tomahawks, quiver and arrows, bows, grinding stones, full headdresses worn by chiefs, and many other items.

Temple spoke many of the Indian dialects fluently as well as Spanish and French.

References:

Oklahoma Today, Autumn 1964, "Temple Houston" by Paul Laune.
"Sand in My Eyes" by Seigniora Russell Laune; Publisher, Copyright.
Strum's Oklahoma Magazine, Vol. 12, No. 2, Pages 20-23, April 1911 "The Brilliant, Eccentric Temple Houston" by Seigniora Russell Laune.
True West, August 1963, "Sam's Youngest Boy" by Frank X. Tolbert.

IX

Trial of a Lonely Cowboy

The attorney for the defense rose from his place at the council table and stepped up to the jury box. Tall, lithe, dark of complexion with brown hair flowing to his shoulders, he presented a picture in striking contrast with the others in the courtroom. He wore a Prince Albert coat, brocaded vest and Spanish style bell-bottomed trousers.

He unfastened his long skirted coat, placed his thumbs in the armholes of his waistcoat and surveyed the men before him. There was a hush of expectancy in the room. One of the most colorful lawyers ever to plead a case in an Indian Territory or Texas court was about to present his case. He was Temple Houston, youngest son of General Sam Houston, sometimes called 'The Raven's Fledgling.'

"Gentlemen of the jury, my client is not a man of arms; he is not an accomplished gunfighter. He has never before used guns, coming as he does from a faraway state to settle amongst us and become a substantial citizen.

"These are the facts in the case. This lately lamented cowboy who was so unfortunately killed by my client in the protection of his own life had the reputation of being a gunfighter of more than ordinary ability. And that, gentlemen, is a dangerous reputation.

"All other men fear such a man and they have a right to fear him. It has been said of the deceased that he could let another man start his draw, that he could even let the other man get his pistol out into his hand, and that he could even then, draw, shoot, and kill his adversary.

45

"My client had heard these things and he feared that gunfighter. I don't blame him. And you don't blame him for not waiting until that known killer could put a bullet through his heart."

In the back of the jury box were two or three veniremen, evidently sons of the soil, who did not appear overly impressed and it was to them that the picturesque lawyer now addressed the fire of his oratory.

"In Oklahoma and Texas," Houston continued, "there are men so accomplished in killing that they can place a gun in the hands of an inexperienced man and shoot him before he can raise the hammer and pull the trigger. Gentlemen of the jury, I will give you a demonstration . . ." The white hands of the lawyer flashed down from the vest, there was a slight flutter of the long coattails and the calm of the courtroom was broken as the two six-shooters went into action, one firing toward the jury box, and the other toward the bench where the judge sat.

Pandemonium set in. The judge ducked quickly behind his bench; the jurors fled from the jury box by way of the nearest exit, whether it be a window or through the crowded courtroom and out the front door. And then all was dead quiet. The lawyer was standing alone with weapons in hand, a boyish grin on his face as he watched the judge pick himself up off the floor. The jurors, after a time, began returning to the box. There was a purplish tinge of anger noticeable on the judge's face.

"Mr. Houston!" he snapped, "It would seem that you have no respect whatever for this court."

"Your Honor, I meant no harm. My revolvers were loaded with blanks. It was merely a demonstration to impress the jurors with the speed that can be accomplished by a practiced gunfighter and to show them what any normal man would do in the face of fear."

The jury was apparently impressed. However, within a few minutes after receiving the judge's instructions, they returned a verdict of guilty against Houston's client.

This did not stop Houston. He filed for a motion for a new trial on the grounds that the law did not permit a jury to scatter during the hearing of a case and mix with the public—and this jury did scatter.

A new trial was granted giving Houston more time to prepare his case and went into court with a better knowledge of both his client, and the crime. He also studied the characters of the jurymen individually until he knew their innermost thoughts. This time his client was acquitted.

Another startling event that happened to the lawyer that seemed always to be in the limelight of action. Temple was in Enid for a trial and after the close of the trial he and Judge O.C. Wybrant were riding horseback down the middle of the street. This was the custom of all noted men of the legal profession because they were less likely to be a target of someone holding a grudge and hiding in wait for them. The conversation was pleasant and neither man was particularly looking for or expecting trouble, although they were always conscious that something could happen.

Temple reined his horse with one hand and in the other held a law book he had used in the day's trial. The law book was of Oklahoma Territory Statutes published in 1893. It was bound in soft tan leather and about four inches thick, containing 1384 pages. In the front of the book was the Declaration of Independence and the Constitution of the United States.

Suddenly a shot rent the air. Aimed at Temple Houston, the bullet found its mark but it was not destined to kill, the law book being the recipient of the spent bullet. It was embedded half way through the huge book at page 654.

Who fired the shot and why was never known.

Since he and Judge Wybrant were close friends, Temple gave him the book that had saved his life and it is now in the possession of the judges' daughter, Mrs. Joy Wybrant Cotton.

On the many trials that took Temple Houston all over the Panhandle during his tenure as district attorney, he had the pleasure of making friends with Judge J.D. Hamlin of Amarillo. Both Houston and the judge were very serious about their law work and wanted to see that justice was done at any cost; also they were just as serious about their pleasure. After the court had adjourned for the day the two arms of the law (and probably at times others) would meet either in Houston's hotel room or at the home of Judge Hamlin.

On one such occasion Temple decided, after both were feeling no pain from their drinks, they began toasting each other and were in general having a jolly good time. Judge Hamlin was at the time living on the third floor of the Elmhurst Hotel in Amarillo. Amarillo having gone dry, the Judge always had a stock of liquor shipped in regularly on mail order so that when he and any of his friends wanted a drink, it was readily available.

On this occasion, two other men were with them. Where they came from or who they were is not known, but they were probably strangers whom, while feeling in a friendly mood, the two asked to join them. They sat quietly on the bed, drinking very little and appearing very amazed at the capacity of the jovial judge and attorney.

Temple had a special way of mixing their drinks, which were drunk from goblet glasses. First, he would put in a spoon of sugar, add a half glass of water, and pour from glass to glass until the sugar had dissolved. Then he would finish filling the glass with whiskey and pour from glass to glass until it was well mixed and divide it equally, the Judge having one and Temple the other. Their conversation was lively and for the most part far above the intellect of the two guests. The door of the room stood slightly ajar.

Suddenly, the door was thrown open widely and there stood, as Judge Hamlin described her, a sweet-faced but determined woman of great beauty and dignity. She stood for a moment, looking in. Temple had his back to the door and could not see the beautiful apparition that had just entered.

"Senator Houston, what do you mean by being in this disreputable company?" Temple immediately turned and setting his undrunk drink, which he called the Houston-Hamlin toddy, on the table, walked forward in the most courtly manner, and bowed gracefully.

"Mrs. Houston, I am delighted to see you," he said.

This trip of Houston's had been excessively long and Mrs. Houston felt that he was spending too much time in the company of his drinking buddies and had not considered coming home. She had taken the train from Woodward to Amarillo to look for him. She was well acquainted with Mr. and Mrs. C.B. Vivian, who owned the Elmhurst Hotel and naturally came there from the train. Mrs. Vivian told her that the errant husband was in the judge's rooms.

References

Enid Oklahoma News, March 17, 1968, Page 4-B.
Ellis County Capital, Magazine Section, March 1951.
Letter from Mrs. Joy Cotton, Enid Oklahoma, June 22, 1974.
The Flamboyant Judge, J.D. Hamlin, as told to J. Evetts Haley and Wm. Curry Holden, Published by Palo Duro Press, 1972 Canyon, Texas. Copyright, Palo Duro Press.

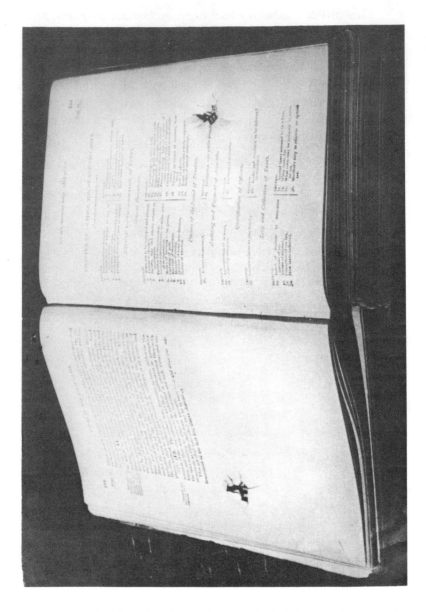

TEMPLE HOUSTON law book that saved his life, note bullet hole.
—*Courtesy Mrs. Joy Cotton, Enid, Oklahoma, reproduced by Cliff's Camera Shop, Enid, Oklahoma.*

X

A New Home in Oklahoma

Temple loved to play with his children and allowed them to play with his prize collection of Indian relics even in his absence. He was never too busy or preoccupied to pass a little time with his own children or with the children of the town. The children loved his pranks and jokes and the never-ending stories he told them. They believed him to be the smartest man alive and often went to him for advice. As for treasures, the walls of his den were lined with these relics and pictures of his idol, 'The Little Corporal,' Napoleon, in battle and in retreat.

Paule Laune recalls that as children, he and his sister played with Richard (called Dick by his friends) and Mary, the youngest Houston children. They did not realize the value of the interesting 'toys' they had to play with until many years later. After the death of Temple Houston, these valuable relics were donated and sold to museums. They included Indian shields, war bonnets, lances, fringed jackets, and even a gold-handled dagger Houston obtained on his trip to the Yucatan. There was also a child's dress made especially for little Mary by the Indians.

Laura was not only a beautiful woman, she was a woman dearly loved by her husband. She lived a quiet life as a housewife and mother but when she and Temple walked down the street together, they always held hands just as young lovers. She spoke with a Louisiana accent that she developed during her early childhood on the plantation where she was born.

Temple was so enamored with his wife that he never ceased to call her his "Valentine," chosen because they were married on Valentine's day. Whenever he was called upon to make a business trip out of town, he never returned home without gifts for her and their children. Her gifts ranged from crystal champagne glasses with eight-inch stems, cut glass punch bowl with cups to serve forty-eight guests, hand-painted plates, and personal items.

Among the many famous people entertained in the Houston home was Carrie Nation. Young Sam became frightened of her when he saw her in her old-fashioned nightcap. It had been arranged that Mrs. Nation would sleep with him, but after viewing this sight so frightening to a small child Sam III refused to allow it. The family felt that by letting him get to sleep first everything would be all right for Mrs. Nation to slip in and sleep in the same bed. Argument and hysteria again reigned the next morning when young Sam awoke first and found the frightening thing soundly sleeping in his bed. With the tact and dignity that was her best characteristic, Mrs. Houston soon had the situation under control. However, Sam III never forgot Mrs. Nation.

The Houstons began plans for their new and permanent home. The wonderlust in Temple had quieted sufficiently for him to want permanent roots and a good home for his family. They had made the plans for a two-story frame house and work had begun. But again things did not run smoothly. It was during one of Temple's circuit court trips that his partner of the time went to as many clients as he could and collected the money due the firm, and without taking out the part that belonged to Houston or even notifying Mrs. Houston of his plans, he took all the money and left town.

When he returned home and found that his partner had left town, he began to do a little checking. This was when he discovered that he was almost penniless. He continued with the building of the house, which was completed late in August, 1898, in time for the family to move just after the birth of little Mary Lea.

There was no Catholic Church in Woodward but there were enough people of that faith that one was needed. Temple began to pull strings, talk to people, and finally obtained enough property for the church building, a parking lot for the buggies, and a hitchrail for the horses. Laura wanted the church built on the corner so that it could be seen from all directions but was overruled by several other ladies and the church was built on the inside of the lot with the parking facilities on the corner. Although Laura did not take an active part in church work after that, her husband spent many hours with the priest assigned to the parish. Father Kamp and Temple became such good friends that later Temple embraced the faith and Father Kamp read the eulogy at his funeral, which was a masterpiece description of the kind of man that Temple Lea Houston was.

Temple was not only favored by his wife and family; most of the ladies he met were immediately enchanted with his personality. Sidney Laune was not married when they first met but when he did marry it was to a Texas girl whom he had courted whenever possible for about two years. No one except his law partner, Judge Dean, even knew he was planning to be married. But the word got around before the couple returned.

This was the perfect opening for Temple to pull one of his practical jokes. When the newly-weds arrived in Woodward after a long and grueling trip, they were met by Temple in the lobby of the hotel as they registered and several other men of the town. They crowded around to meet the lovely new bride.

Temple was the first to step forward and introduce himself. Mrs. Laune was immediately impressed with his charm and good looks. She remarked later, "As I placed my hand in his I felt an instant liking."

As he stood holding her hand he began to tease her about her husband, retelling with delight an incident that happened on one of their trips together.

As he began to tell the story the other men crowded closer, knowing that they were in for a dramatic recounting of a tale they had heard often before. But I must repeat the exact words of Mrs. Laune or risk losing the delight with which Temple told the tired but polite and charming lady about her husband.

"As he stood with his hand in mine," wrote Seignora Russell Laune, he recounted with relish the story of their trip from Beaver City where they had gone on the district court circuit; Mr. Laune was driving a new team of broncos to his buggy.

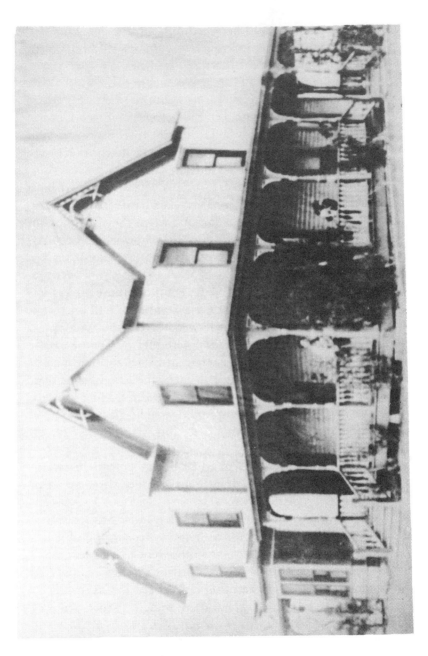

HOME of the Temple Houston family, Woodward, Oklahoma.
—*Courtesy of Sam Houston Museum, Huntsville, Texas.*

" 'I kept telling Laune it was important for me to get to Woodward as soon as possible' said Houston, 'but he refused to hurry the horses. Noon came, and Laune stopped the team and began to unhitch them from the buggy. I remonstrated in fervid eloquence, but to no purpose. Laune hung nosebags from their ears and never did two animals take more time to munch their grain. Then gentlemen, heaven help me if he didn't start to picket them out to graze! He said they were too tired to continue the journey—they needed rest and grass. After expending my breath in futile argument, I stretched out on the prairie, pulled my hat over my brow, and prepared to sleep.

" 'Suddenly there was the most frightful ripping and snorting. I looked up to see those poor weary animals that needed refreshment and rest, tearing over the peaceful landscape as though all the furies of Hades were driving them. S.B. was standing there with a hurt, baffled look on his face, watching them go. With harness flying they high-tailed it into the far blue distance.

" 'And I said, I hope to God those poor jaded beasts get some rest and grass! Then I closed my eyes and went to sleep. While I slept there in the shade of the buggy, S.B. trudged over the prairie, through the blistering heat, after those da— durned horses. He caught them somewhere, cornered in a pasture, or they'd be running yet.' "

In another incident where Sidney Laune, Temple Houston, and two other men had been to another town on court business and were returning home, they ran into a little trouble. The Canadian River is noted for its turbulence at the best, and at this time it had been raining for several days and the river was swollen to the banks. In most places it was impassable. It was roaring down stream in a torrent of swift rapids and currents.

Picking the most likely place for a crossing, the men decided on taking a chance, all of them wanting to get home and out of the cold, damp weather. Working their frightened team into the swirling water, they began to make slow progress, but they had to keep a strong rein on the team. Suddenly a log hit the back of the hack, breaking it loose from the team. The horses scrambled and fought their way to safety and when on the opposite bank they made fast pace away from the frightening ordeal they had been through.

The four men finally managed to reach the security of the bank and upon assuring themselves that none were hurt, only drenched to the skin, they sat down to rest and regain their strength before starting out for other means of travel. In the stillness, broken only by the roar of the river as it fought its way downstream taking along all the debris it could accumulate, and the heavy breathing of the exhausted men, only one ventured to speak. Temple was more than drenched, he was angry.

"The Mississippi may be the father of all rivers but the Canadian is damn sure the mother-in-law," he fumed.

On one of his quieter days, Temple could be found in the saloon enjoying a few drinks and good conversation with his friends.

On one particular day, several young boys had decided to go fishing. Not having any bait they decided to dig up some worms. They had secured only a few of the wriggly little fish teasers when one of the boys turned over a rock and found a salamander resting there. Not knowing what it was, they decided to take it to Temple Houston. He would know, after all he knew everything. Looking around until they found a can and a strong stick, they then pushed the salamander into the can. Instinct told them not to handle it.

They hurried down the hill toward town and looked into every saloon until they reached the right one in their search for the man they considered to know everything. Taking the can inside they asked him what it was.

"Why boys, what you have there is a very rare specimen of a Huajalote (pronounced wa-ha-lo-te and means turkey in Spanish) you should take very good care of this and preserve it." Temple told them. "Go to the drugstore and get some alcohol to put it in."

"But we don't have any money."

"Here" and Temple tossed them a quarter. "And if there is anything left buy yourselves some candy."

Delighted the boys rushed off to the drugstore to get the alcohol to preserve their rare find.

Temple had begun to suffer an occasional but severe headache but not wanting his friends and family to think him incapable of work, took the train to Oklahoma City to see a doctor. His advice was to take life easier and to slack off from his work and drinking. This Temple could not do. If duty called, he must do his best and give all of himself to his client. If the children demanded his attention, he could not refuse. He could not let his loving wife know of the seriousness of his trouble and cause her undue trouble. He firmly believed the headaches would pass and all would be well.

There were series of events that began to occur that caused his friends some concern. Since Temple would not confide in them, his friends did not know if he was drinking heavier or if he was ill. He lost his temper over nothing, only to regret it deeply moments later. There were times when the headaches would hit him so severely that he would have to hold onto something, such as a hitch rail, the rail surrounding the jury box, or his desk until the headaches subsided somewhat. Friends said they only seemed to last a few minutes and he was his fun-loving, witty, and cunning self again.

One serious incident that stemmed from the pain occurred when Temple Jr. went to get his pony that had been pastured for the winter on the farm of a Joe B. Jenkins. With his friend who accompanied him, Temple Jr. started to ride off on his pony only to be stopped by Jenkins. He was told that he could not have the pony until Jenkins was paid for the winter grazing.

Temple Jr., called Pokey by his friends, said that his father would pay him next time Jenkins was in town. Not good enough, Jenkins wanted the money before releasing the pony. Pokey called him some names and Jenkins slapped the boy's face and told him to get off his land.

Of course, Temple Jr. told his father of the whole incident. It is doubtful that he held back any of his part in the fracas since he was one of the many children who admired and trusted Temple Houston and thought of him as the cure of all evil.

Several days passed before anything came of it. Jenkins came into town and was riding down the street. Houston crossed over to him and asked, "Is your name Jenkins?"

"Yes, it is."

Thereupon, Temple drew his pistol and shot Jenkins twice, telling him that would teach him to manhandle his son. Jenkins swayed in the saddle, but did not fall. He turned toward Houston.

"Houston, you are a bad man," and with that remark turned his horse and went to the drugstore of Dr. Thomas who called in Dr. J.M. Workman. Jenkins was patched up and recovered nicely from his wounds.

Houston was tried and found guilty of assault with intent to kill. He was fined $500 and ordered to get his hair cut. As far as could be found in the records, neither was complied with and no one in office seemed very inclined to push the enforcement of the court ruling. It would not seem to be out of fear of Houston that they held back, but out of respect for his full life of supporting the law and their respect and friendship for him.

His headaches began to occur more frequently. He purchased a heavy coat with a beaver collar to protect his neck against the cold prairie wind, and this helped to eliminate the seriousness of the headaches.

References

Oklahoma Today, Autumn 1964, "Temple Houston," by Paul Laune.

"Sand in My Eyes" by Seigniora Russell Laune; Publisher, J.P. Lippincott Company, Philadelphia and New York, Copyright 1965 by author. Printed in U.S.A. Library of Congress Cat. No. 56-6420.,

Strum's Oklahoma Magazine, Vol. 12, No. 2, Pages 20-23, April 1911, "The Brilliant, Eccentric Temple Houston" by Seigniora Russell Laune.

True West, August, 1963 "Sam's Youngest Boy" by Frank Z. Tolbert.

Letter to Mrs. Grace Longino Cox, Sam Houston Museum from C.R. Hayhurst, Courtesy of Sam Houston Museum and C.R. Hayhurst.

XI

Gunfire And Death

In mid 1895, the extremely hot weather may have caused tempers to flare more readily.

A case was on trial in Justice Williams' court alleging that several young men had stolen a keg of beer from the Santa Fe Railroad Company. Legal counsel were Temple Houston, who was on retainer as the railroad company lawyer, County Attorney B.B. Smith, for the prosecution, and the firm of Jennings and Jennings, John and Ed, for the defendants.

As usual, when Houston appeared in court the courtroom was crowded beyond capacity. Spectators were sitting in windows and in the aisles, so close that the sweat of one permeated with another, exhausting the very oxygen needed to breath.

One of the Jennings attorneys called opposing counsel liars and as tempers flared Temple Houston returned the compliment. Guns were brought into view. Friends of the Jenningses grabbed the two men, wresting the guns from their grasp. The Houston faction and city officials reacted by coming between the opposing counsel and taking "Old Betsy" from Temple. This was the beginning of openly expressed bad blood between Houston and the Jennings family. Friends of both sides later admitted that they had heard Ed Jennings say that he would "get" Temple Houston yet.

Jack Love had come to Woodward at the opening of the strip too, having been appointed by Territorial Governor Renfro to act as sheriff of the territory. He was also the Democratic nominee for representative of the County of Woodward to the legislature, but was defeated by only two votes by the Republican nominee, G.W. Gradfield.

59

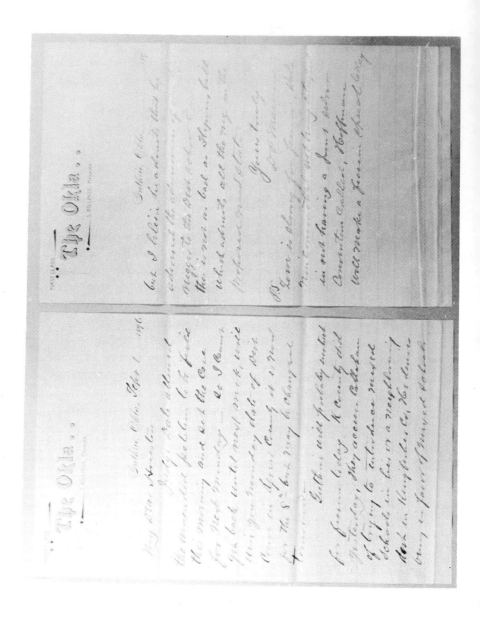

LETTER to Houston from law partner D.P. Marum. —*Reproduced from aged original by Ben Pilcher, Abilene, Texas.*

On September 20th of that year, another case was brought to court involving the same attorneys. Frank Garst, defendant, had accused John E. (Jack) Love and J.T. Ward of illegally fencing government land, charging other ranchers fees to graze their cattle there, and for water rights that actually belonged to the people. This case brought out many delays and was not finally settled until October 8, 1898. The defendant changed lawyers twice during this interim.

Al Jennings later wrote in his book, "Through the Shadows with O. Henry," that Jack Love had tried to bribe his brother to drop the Garst case but his brother refused. He also stated that he had not gotten angry when Houston had stated loudly and openly in court that he was grossly ignorant of the law. But he did admit on other pages of the book that for the most part of his life his temper had ruled his decisions and that was the reason that he had been in so much trouble. And that he heard that Ed was dead and blamed his unbridled temper for causing the trouble. His version differs in every way from that of all the other witnesses and court records.

The Garst trial was delayed and in the interim the trouble between the Jenningses and Houston erupted, forcing Garst to change lawyers to the firm of Laune and Dean.

During the first hearing, Judge J.D.F. Jennings presided with Houston and his law partner, Robert J. Ray, representing Love and Ward, and the Jennings firm of John and Ed representing Garst. Al Jennings paid a visit to his father from El Reno where he was practicing law and took an active part in the trial because of the enmity between Houston and his brother Ed.

It seemed to Temple that the judge was favoring his sons. Now, such a situation would not be allowed as a judge so closely connected with attorneys for either side would have to disqualify himself; but at that time judges were called upon to serve a larger territory and no other judge was available.

In making a point for the cause of their client, Al Jennings evidently overstepped his legal jurisdiction.

"Your Honor, this man is grossly ignorant of the law," Temple shouted as he jumped to his feet.

Again guns flashed; again friends and officials intervened and prevented bloodshed in the courtroom. Court was adjourned for the day and the case was not again to appear on court dockets until December of that year.

This incident was not so easily smoothed over by friends. All of the Jennings family except Frank were involved, and all with high tempers, were angry and ready for a settlement of the argument, even if it meant bloodshed. They retired to their law office to discuss the situation. Tempers still hot, the boys felt the office should be guarded for fear Houston and his friends would try to break in and do damage. The judge was old and mature enough to want to avoid a fight, if possible, but did agree that Ed and John should stay in town. Since Al had been the worst troublemaker of them all and he was the one who had been insulted in open court, he should accompany the judge to the farm. How wrong the judge was when he felt he had evaded further violence by this.

The night was hot and sultry. The prairie winds were blowing up little dust whirls only to die down to sudden stillness. Temple and Jack Love had in the meantime discussed Temple's safety and Love offered to stay with his friend to give added protection in case of trouble. Temple refused his help but they retired to Jack Garvey's Cabinet Saloon for a few drinks and to listen to the music. Temple was a great lover of music and never missed a chance to listen. Love left, but stayed in the shadows just outside the side door where he could see his friend as well as the front door. Temple, unafraid as he was, stood leaning with his elbow on the piano, the better to appreciate the music. Neither of the men appeared worried.

John and Ed Jennings arrived, saw Houston, and reached for their guns.

"I wouldn't do that," Temple admonished. Neither of the Jennings listened to the warning. Guns roared, bullets flew, the lights were shot out, and pandemonium set in. Jack Love and Temple fired at the same time, both shots hitting their mark. Ed Jennings' bullet lodged in the piano just under Temple's arm. When the firing was over Ed Jennings lay dead on the floor and John had a bullet in his upper left arm. John ran from the saloon yelling for someone to give him a gun.

Houston and Love were unscathed. All guns were almost empty. Houston and Love went immediately to Sheriff Bob Benn to surrender their weapons and themselves.

Inquest was held October 8, 1895, in Woodward County Courthouse to determine the cause of death and persons responsible in the death of Ed Jennings.

J.M. Workman, coroner, presided and Paul J. McLeod, H.C. Thompson, J.M. Slaybough, R.B. Clark, Joe Hedrick, and Foreman Joseph Finley were the jurors.

The verdict was that Ed Jennings came to his death from gunshot wounds received during the process of a fight in Garvey's Cabinet Saloon, in which himself, John Jennings, Temple Houston, and Jack Love were participants.

Houston, charged with manslaughter, and Love, charged with assault with intent to kill, were bound over for trial with bond set at $5000 each. They posted bond and were freed.

One newspaper stated that the evidence showed that Ed Jennings was shot twice through the head and from the range, it appeared that his brother, John, must have fired the fatal shot. This is an important feature, although circumstantial. The witnesses would not or could not bear up the statement. To add to this, the case of the prosecution was weak, being hampered by the feeling that the killing was justifiable. County Attorney B.B. Smith was assisted by Shannon McCray in the prosecution and the defense lawyers were Henry E. Asp, D.P. Marum, Robert J. Ray, and Roy Hoffman. With the lack of modern facilities such as balistics tests and pathology tests many of these suppositions had to remain just that. There was also the possibility that the fatal bullet came from the gun of Jack Love or from a bystander who chose to take part in the fracas for some unknown reason.

If this is what Houston and Love believed then Houston must have given his friend and benefactor some sage legal advice as they walked alone to Sheriff Benn's office. With Houston the killer, it would be self defense since the Jenningses fired first and with good legal counsel he could get off. With Love, however, it would have been a different situation and he could be convicted of first-degree murder. At that early stage of the situation, it is possible that neither of them thought that the bullet might have been from John's gun or from a participating bystander. This was never proved, in fact, the only mention of it was in the newspaper previously mentioned.

Trial was held in District Court in Woodward County, Oklahoma, on May 15, 1896. Walter E. Younger gave testimony in a deposition before Shannon McCray, probate judge of Woodward County, and this was admitted into evidence. Walter Younger was a printer and was in the newspaper office just a short distance from the saloon when the shooting occurred. He gave testimony that John Jennings ran from the back door of the saloon and yelled for someone to give him a gun, indicating that his was either empty or had been dropped when he had been shot. He also testified that Jennings stopped and talked to someone that he thought was a character known as "Handsome Harry" and not a very well respected person. Not having seen the actual shooting, he could not testify as to who had fired the first shot or how the parties of the shooting were situated in the saloon.

Other witnesses called were J.M. Workman, John Garvey, saloon owner, and Leon J. Pitts, who testified that he had heard Ed Jennings say he was out to get Temple Houston. Also testifying was Pink Ellis, who swore that in an earlier conversation with Ed, John, and Al Jennings they stated that the trouble with Temple Houston was not over yet and he had better look out.

When the trial was over and the jury had reached a verdict, George O. Bailey, jury foreman, read the verdict to the court and a large crowd of spectators—verdict—NOT GUILTY.

One newspaper article stated that Temple Houston later received a letter from the Jennings family admitting that he had done the only possible thing to save his life and advised Temple to go his way and they would go theirs. They held no grudge. No such letter was found in Houston's files after his death.

Al Jennings, however, continued to spread the unsupported tales as he stated in his book, 'Through The Shadows With O'Henry,' that Houston and Love ran from justice and that he caught up with them in the badlands and lectured them for fifteen minutes, but saw they still would not surrender their guns and go back for trial. He also stated that he drew his guns and killed both before they could draw, that Houston was plainly afraid of him.

Houston died in 1905 and Love lived to the age of ninety and died in Oklahoma City. Close friends of Houston state positively that he was not afraid of anything, man or beast, and he would brave the devil in his own lair. It seems unlikely that Al Jennings, known as the "half-pint bad man," being only five feet tall, would brace two men well known to be good with their guns and both measuring over six feet tall.

References

Personal interview, Clark R. Hayhurst, August 1972.
Oklahoma Times Journal, October 10, 1895, Page 1, Cols. 5-6.
Court Records, Woodward County, Oklahoma.
Sam Houston Museum, Huntsville, Texas (files on Temple Houston).
The South and West, Beaver Oklahoma, Thursday, May 21, 1896, Page 1, Col. 6.

TEMPLE LEA HOUSTON about age 40, as a successful lawyer and
orator. —*Courtesy of Mrs. Mary Henderson, reproduced by Austin
Camera Shop, Abilene, Texas.*

XII

Legal Skulduggery

Temple Houston used every means of legal structure, every course open to him to defend a client and was not above a little legal skullduggery if it benefited his client.

Such was the case of Tom O'Hare, Texas Ranger, accused of killing an Indian. There were not witnesses but the circumstantial evidence leading up to the crime was strong enough to prove no one else could have killed the Indian.

It happened when O'Hare came from Mobeetie, about sixty miles west across the state line in Texas to see about some cattle he owned. He was known as "Red Tom" because of his flaming red hair. When sober he was a likeable sort but when drunk he became overbearing.

He arrived in Cheyenne, Oklahoma, on November 18, 1893, stabled his horse, and spent the night drinking and carousing from saloon to saloon. By morning he was well inebriated and began trying to pick a fight. He went into Thurmond Brothers Store where the brothers, later well-known bankers and ranchers, were talking to John B. Harrison and Oscar Cassidy. At the counter was an Indian named Wolf Hair, who was making a few purchases. Red Tom began cursing the Indian who, although he could not speak English, understood that trouble was brewing from the tone of O'Hare's voice.

As Harrison and Cassidy started to leave in disgust, Wolf Hair darted out the door, jumped in his wagon, and rode out of town as fast as the team could go.

Red Tom raced after him waving his Winchester.

"There's going to be a killing," remarked Frank Hunt to his brother, Irving.

As both men disappeared over the ridge two shots were heard. A few minutes later, O'Hare galloped back to town and told a group of waiting citizens, "There's a dead Indian over the hill and if he's shot above the left eye, he is my Indian."

He surrendered his gun to Sheriff "Skillity" Bill Johnson. Several Indians who were in town took charge of the body.

Fearing another Indian uprising, several citizens of Cheyenne rode to surrounding towns with the warning. Word got out somehow that the Indian was caught stealing cattle. U.S. troops were called in. Fear reigned over the land. From several newspaper accounts, the story varied in most details even to the Indian's name, which in one account was Chief Red Blanket and in another story he was called Bob Tail.

Eighty-four Indians under the leadership of White Shield and Mike Big Bear came to Cheyenne to demand possession of the prisoner. By using all the diplomacy at his call, Joe Purdy, who was on friendly terms with the Indians, convinced them that they could not release Red Tom as he was being held for trial for murder. They returned home to await the trial.

Temple Houston, Red Tom's attorney, requested a change of venue on the grounds that feelings were running high and O'Hare could not get a fair trial. This was not entirely the reason for the requested change of venue, the main reason being that recently a trial was held in El Reno where two young Araphahoes were charged with killing two white settlers. The Indians claimed public feeling was against them in this trial. Houston felt that if a white man was tried in El Reno for killing an Indian he would be acquitted. He was right. The minds of the public could still remember earlier astrocities committed by Indians.

With Judge John H. Burford presiding, defense attorneys were Houston and Ray of Woodward and Bush and Grigsby of El Reno. Houston led the defense. Prosecution was led by J.W. McMurtry, assisted by Gillette and Brown of Oklahoma City. County Attorney Roger Mills acted as advisor.

Judge Brown led the final pleading for the prosecution in a brilliant speech. He had the jury almost won over to a man. But when Houston began speaking for the defense, Ben Hayes, the bailiff, whispered to Judge Brown, "Judge, he's got your man and gone with him."

After deliberating from Monday night, December 3, 1894, at eleven until Wednesday noon, the jury issued a verdict of "not guilty."

The judge admonished O'Hare that for his own safety he should stay out of Oklahoma.

Another classic account where Houston used a little legal skullduggery was in the defense of Alfred Son, charged with murder.

George Weightman, known as "Red Buck," was to come to his rescue. Red Buck sent Temple a message as soon as he learned that Houston was the defense attorney that if he would meet him without escort of the law he would divulge information that would prove the innocence of his client. Red Buck was the most noted and feared outlaw of that part of the country, known for wantonly killing just for the sole pleasure of killing.

Temple Houston, with many friends among the lawless as well as the lawabiding, was not one to look a gift horse in the mouth. He sent word back that he would meet Red Buck at the designated place and time with only a driver in his company. He assured Red Buck that he knew the place and that no one would know of their meeting.

Temple hired a young man known only as Johnny as his driver and headed for the rendezvous. Johnny was not as brave as he could have been and when told of their destination was all for turning back but the fee for driving the buckboard was not a bad means of income, so he silently prayed for their safety and drove on.

It was hot, even in the late afternoon. Johnny's fear contributed to the sweat on the hot reins, the beads of sweat on his face. On the other hand, Temple was calm and in complete control of his emotions.

They drove across the prairie lands where there were no wagon ruts. This too disturbed Johnny.

"Outlaws don't strive to be accessible, son," Houston said, "They don't anticipate being visited very often."

The going was rough for a time and Johnny held on tightly to the buckboard with one hand and the reins with the other. Houston bounced along with the buckboard as smoothly and lightly as if he had been sitting in a rocking chair.

"No need to hurry, son," Houston admonished, "Mr. Weightman doesn't plan for us to arrive until it is quite dark."

"Sir, if you don't mind my asking, what do you plan on doing when we get there?"

Puffing on his cigar Houston said, "Well, son, since you're my associate in this venture you have a right to know something about it.

"I engaged your services to drive and my profession gives words priority over guns so you won't need the gun in the back that you brought along."

Johnny showed his surprise; he had tried to hide the gun.

"Mr. Weightman did not invite me out for a gun fight. He has some information concerning a trial coming up soon."

They came over a rise and could see Red Buck's campfire. They were just coming up to the fire when out of the darkness came a voice, "Hold it! Right there! You Temple Houston?"

"Correct, and I suppose I am addressing Mr. Weightman."

"You suppose right. Got a gun on you?"

"No gun."

Red Buck came around and stood in front of them.

"Who is he?"

"Just the young man I commissioned to drive me. If you are through with your inquisition, kindly put the gun down. It makes the boy nervous."

After some light conversation about horses they sat down by the fire. Red Buck poured them some coffee and then began telling Houston his story.

"I hear they got some guy in jail for shooting Fred Hoffman."

"Alfred Son, I'm doing my best to defend him."

"Yeah, I know," Red Buck stirred the coals and leaned closer to Houston. "Son never killed Hoffman, I done it."

"Would you care to swear to that here and now?"

"I swear to it."

"Thank you, sir, for your hospitality and your help in the case."

"Will that get him off?"

"I think Mr. Son will live now; soothe your troubled soul."

On the basis of Red Buck's clandestine testimony Houston constructed his defense of Alfred Son.

The courtroom at El Reno, Oklahoma, was packed that November 16, 1897, when Temple Houston gave his summation in the trial of Alfred Son, charged with murder. This was the third time Alfred Son had been tried for the same offense, each time to have it appealed. Houston first reviewed the facts of the case as presented by both sides then launched into the close of his plea for his client with the following words:

"Gentlemen, as I told you in the beginning, the territory has shown no motive for the commission of such a crime, and we have given you a reasonable—a true—explanation of every act and utterance of the defendant—even for his trip in that fatal direction. He went only to woo (and win) one of the daughters of the land, tender-eyed, and fair to look upon; and how like a boy, to take the shortest route to see his sweetheart, and seeing her, take her back by the longest route. The life of this boy, up to the instant of his accusation, has been faultless; and do you believe that he took this sudden and awful plunge from innocence into fathomless depths of crime—from childlike purity into hideous murder? When asked to believe such a supposition, refer to your duties, as given you in his honor's charge; apply the law as there laid down to the proof, and then follow the dicatates of your conscience, and I do not fear the result. This brave boy asks me to say to you that, to him, honor is dearer than life, and as the old exemplar of purest patriotism thundered in the ears of his country's oppressors, he says in this, his hour of trial, "Give me liberty or give me death." He demands that you free him or inflict the death penalty. Rather than that you should fix upon his boyish brow the brand of felon, he would prefer to walk from your presence with his body polluted with the scales of whitest leprosy. He appeals to no sentiment of pity, only to the justice of his country's laws, which you are so solemnly charged to administer. You came into that box with light hearts and conscience clear. Oh, may you leave there thus! Untortured with the curse of having wrecked the life of him whose life you hold in the hollow of your hands. And he is so young, too. Boyhood's down still softens upon his child-like face. You will not be here long now. Your homes where loved ones are even now watching, waiting, to greet you, and when you clasp them to your manly breasts may the rapture at that moment be not embittered by the memory of having wrecked the life of yonder boy, whom all law and righteousness plead with you to save. Gentlemen, be just; heed not the perjured fiends who thirst for this boys blood, and in the years yet to come, when the pale messenger summons you before the court where you shall be tried along side of kings of the earth, each memoried hour of life shall come back to you with awful distinctness and then happily you can recall that when you judged here, you judged with justice, and in the very spirit of Him who said, 'Even as you did it unto the least of these, so you did it unto me.' So that in the perfection of righteousness you tried the stranger within your gates (for he never saw one of you until he fearlessly placed his fate in your hands) even as you would be tried yourselves. He has a Texas home far across the southern prairies, where the skies wear a deeper purple, where the dawn has a brighter glow and the sunset wears a softer gold; where midnight stars look down upon us in a more unspeakable splendor. His loved ones, like yours, are waiting—no! no! not like yours—for his life is darkened even now by the awful shadow of death; and who shall tell what he feels? Gentlemen, break that suspense; dry those tears; bind up these almost broken hearts, for now no power but you can do so. This noble duty done and each hour of life thereafter will grow proud with this recollection.''

This was Alfred Son's third and final trial. He was freed.

References

Elk City Daily News, Elk City Oklahoma, by Nat M. Taylor, date unknown from a collection held by Mrs. Mary Henderson, San Antonio, Texas.

Plains Indians & Historical Museum, Houston Files, Woodward Oklahoma.

XIII

His Final Work

Oklahoma Territory was fast developing. Many of the leaders in politics and attorneys at law were working toward the Territory becoming a state. Temple Houston and his law partners were very active in this movement. Many of the leaders were aiming their speeches and correspondence toward Temple becoming the first state governor after statehood was granted.

On January 19, 1895, Houston and W.C. Cunningham went to Guthrie in the interest of the stock raisers of the Territory. His commanding appearance and flowing hair attracted attention of everyone they met. His eloquence of speech captivated all with whom he spoke and by the time they left Guthrie, to a man, all were for Temple Houston in any capacity he would serve them. D.P. Marum, one of Temple's partners, wrote to tell him that Judge Dale had altered the amended petition and the case was set for the following Monday. He did not mention what the petition was about but did mention that a Mr. Callahan was trying to introduce mixed schools and that this might deter the admission of the territory into the union.

Although Houston had become embittered with politics in Texas, he was willing to have his name put on the ballot primarily with the hope of preventing the same strategy to become prevalent in the Oklahoma government.

Courtroom dramatics and personal feelings were still strong points in his character. One man went so far as to remind him of his heritage and ability to convince him that he would be elected on the first ballot.

"Besides your ability in holding the attention of a crowd,

you already have your platform," he said. "All you have to do is tell them that you are Sam Houston's son."

"Any man who cannot stand on his own merits does not deserve the position of such honor," Houston thereupon stormed out of the meeting.

Once in the defense of a client being tried for murder, he was reminded of his famous father and urged to use his name to secure freedom for his client. Houston spoke with his usual calm and stated firmly, "My father is not defending this poor unfortunate soul, I am; and I will defend him on the basis of the facts in the case and that I truly believe him to be innocent and on nothing else."

By 1904, Woodward was intoxicated with the thought that their favorite, eccentric, flambouyant Temple Houston stood a good chance to become the first governor. Feeling for this was mounting all across the territory.

But fate took a hand.

For several years, Temple had suffered from severe headaches. At times, they would occur suddenly while he was in court. He would be forced to hold onto something and be very quiet until the severeness of the pain subsided. He had purchased a winter coat with a beaver collar to protect him from the bitter cold winds on his neck and ward off at least some of the headaches.

In his troubled mind and severe pain, he still remembered others less fortunate than himself. One bitter cold day he was walking down the street with Sidney Laune when a beggar stopped them and asked for money for a hot meal. Temple reached into his pocket and handed the man a ten dollar bill.

"Temple, that was a ten," Laune reprimanded, "he could have as easily gotten a hot meal for less than a dollar."

"Then maybe he can get a warm place to sleep tonight," Temple answered as he looked over his shoulder at the man. The beggar was huddled against the wall to protect himself from a sudden gust of wind. His ragged coat was of little help. Temple immediately took off his expensive fur-trimmed coat, walked back to the man, and wrapped it around his shoulders. Without a word he rejoined his friend.

"Now Temple, that coat was too much. You needed that coat as badly as he did, if not worse."

"Oh, S.B., I can get another one at Garvey's for a quarter."

"But the cold wind on your neck!"

"I'll buy a wool scarf too; don't worry, I'll be all right."

A short time later tragedy struck. In the middle of the night a blood vessel burst in that magnificent brain and partially paralyzed the forty-four year old man who was so vibrant and active. The pain was excrutiating. The Woodward doctors had never treated a case similar to this and told Mrs. Houston that all they could do was give him sedatives to ease the pain.

He was moved to the Santa Fe Hospital in Topeka, Kansas, where the verdict was confirmed. Nothing could be done. Love and constant care was all that could be done for him. He lingered for almost a year after that. When the end was near, he was brought home. By this time he was fully paralyzed and almost blind.

On August 15, 1905, he died quietly in his home in Woodward, Oklahoma, among the family he had cherished. He was only forty-five years and three days old. Much too short a life span for the brilliant mind to expound all of its wealth of life and knowledge.

If one would read closely his speech on astronomy, he will see that Temple Lea Houston forsaw much of the space travel and research that man has done in recent years. He would see that Houston believed that the stars and moon were made for man to enjoy and did not believe we should question God's gift to us.

Temple Lea Houston was buried in Laurel Land Cemetery, Woodward, Oklahoma. Twenty-eight years later, his nephew, Temple Houston Morrow, gave a beautiful and moving dedication of the memorial tower and chimes at this cemetery.

Father Kamp, in his funeral tribute, told a crowded gathering, "If we could gather around his coffin all of those who have experienced his goodness, there would not be enough room for them. And what would be the effusions of those whom he delivered from the chains of prison or from an ignominious death?

"It would behoove all of us who have been touched by this life to try to become a great and useful citizen as he was, and imitate him in all he has done for the good of the community."

References

Plains Indian & Historical Museum, Files on Temple Lea Houston, Woodward, Oklahoma.

Strum's Oklahoma Magazine, Vol. 12, No. 2, Pages 20-23, April 1911 "The Brilliant, Eccentric Temple Houston" by Seigniora Russell Laune.

XIV

Aftermath

A brilliant life had been cut short in the death of Temple Lea Houston, but profiteers could not let him rest in peace as he so richly deserved. They garnered from the misuse of his name as they had done to many other outstanding men before him, and since, tearing down the good with spicy, untrue tales to make the story sell quicker and be more fascinating.

About 1934, a magazine published a story about Temple Lea Houston that was not only untrue, for the most part, but it was libelous in the very text. R.C. Crane, writer for the Amarillo *Sunday Globe News*, and a student of history, read the story. He wrote the magazine, calling attention to the many false statements and suggesting a retraction. He sent a copy of the letter to one of the Houston relatives, who in turn mailed the information to Mrs. Laura Houston, widow of the libeled man.

When no retraction was printed, Mrs. Houston filed a damage suit against the magazine. The publisher of the magazine denied having received any communication on the story. Crane was summoned to testify. The jury awarded Mrs. Houston twenty thousand dollars damages, and the other suits involving the children were settled out of court.

This was not the beginning nor the end of the flagrant misuse of the name of Houston. By other writers, he has been described as an outlaw, gunman, anything but the brilliant, law-abiding attorney he was. R.C. Crane, George Turner, Paul Laune, and his mother, Seigniora Russell Laune, were some of the few writers who struggled for accuracy in all that they wrote about him.

Al Jennings, in his book, "Through the Shadows with

O'Henry," claimed that after his brother, Ed Jennings, was killed in Woodward that he chased Houston and Love into the badlands and that they were deathly afraid of him. Further points of his inaccuracy in his book have been discussed previously and proof given that Temple Lea Houston died peacefully in his home in 1905 instead of at the gun of Al Jennings in May of 1896.

As if all of the publicity and heartache to the lonely widow was not enough, she loaned some very valuable items that belonged to her husband to a museum to display in an open house celebration to raise money to expand the museum. These items were some that were too valuable to donate in her reduced financial circumstances. These included a jewel encrusted dagger he had obtained in the Yucatan and was valued at several thousand dollars. A Mr. Thorburson was responsible for returning the collection safely to Mrs. Houston.

However, when she tried to get her collection, he claimed the dagger had been stolen and not recovered, although the boy who was supposed to have stolen it was in the reformatory. The rest had been moved to the museum in Oklahoma City without her permission. In the personal effects of Mrs. Mary Henderson a letter from Mrs. Houston to the Historical Society was found explaining this, but no response was found. It is not known if she ever received her property or payment. Mary was at the time living with her grandmother in Corpus Christi and was not sure of the outcome and no proof was found either way. One museum had offered her a very good price for the collection but did want it intact before making payment. Mr. Thorburson's negligence caused Mrs. Houston to lose the sale, and at the time the money was badly needed to support her family.

The Houston family has been besieged by people wanting to write about and seeking the personal touch about Temple Lea Houston, even though the personal touch was rarely used.

A television series, short lived though it was, did much damage to the brilliant man's memory. Temple Houston Morrow, nephew of Temple Lea Houston, wrote the television producer, Jack Webb, concerning the show offering more and accurate information on his uncle, with full intentions of preserving accuracy in this protrayal and not asking for payment. His response was that they had all of the information they needed—much of which was inaccurate. He was portrayed as an itinerate gun-slinging lawyer with a glib tongue. The only thing that family and friends agreed about on the show was that the star, Jeffrey Hunter, had a slight resemblance to Houston. A vein of sentiment displayed in his endearing term—My Valentine—for his wife and his romping in play with his children was vague and not at all elaborated upon. It failed in that in displaying his characteristics of being innately gentle, non-conformist, the soul of the wonderlust, trustful and honest, it came out that he was flagrant in his use of the law and went out in search of clients. This he never had to do. His popularity was such that he practiced at the beck and call of the people of four states.

Edna Ferber wrote a book based on some of the points of his character. At the time she was interviewing the family, she left the impression that she was doing a factual biography. Instead, when it was published her book was fictional with the main character a composite of several men. Both Temple and his father were used in the characterization, according to Miss Ferber.

After Temple's death, Laura became very close to one of her good friends and neighbors, Mrs. Lige Roberts, known affectionately by the children as 'Aunt Lem.' In later years, Mrs. Roberts wrote to Mary, the youngest child, about her association with Laura. In one letter, she stated that she and Laura would often walk in the late afternoon down to the church and sit on the steps and talk for some time. It was in these moments of close friendship with Mrs. Roberts that Laura was able to live with the grief and loss of her beloved husband. Mrs. Roberts described her as a "Southern belle," who "reigned in New Orleans and Houston with more charm than any other girl you or I have ever known."

Laura Houston went on to serve fourteen years as postmistress of Woodward, an appointment probably obtained partially through her husband's fame, friends, and associates. She remained in the Houston home along with her son, Richard, and his wife, Elizabeth, until her death by heart attack on Easter Sunday, April 17, 1938. She was seventy-three years old. She never remarried after Temple's death.

"It was a good and exciting life," she often said.

References

Letter from Mrs. Lige Roberts to Mrs. Mary Henderson, Oct. 14, 1939.

Strum's Oklahoma Magazine, Vol. 12, No. 2, Pages 20-23, April 1911, "The Brilliant, Eccentric Temple Houston," by Seigniora Russell Laune.

Sam Houston Museum, Huntsville, Texas, files on Temple Lea Houston.

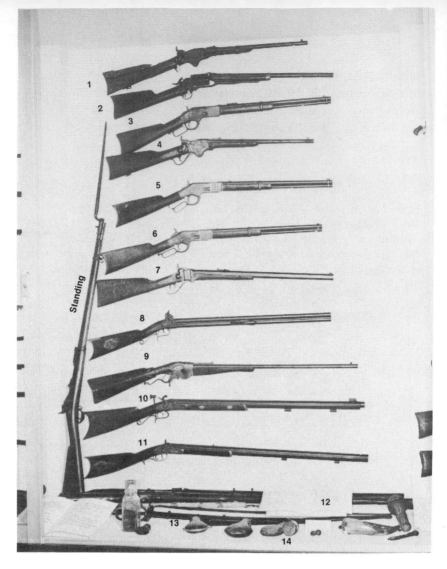

PART of gun collection—standing, Springfield 45-70 Trapdoor, about 1870-80. Top to bottom: 1. Spencer Repeating rifle; 2. Colt Revolving Carbine; 3. Winchester Carbine saddle rifle; 4. Spencer Repeating rifle; 5. Winchester Carbine saddle rifle; 6. Saddle rifle; 7. Evans Repeating rifle; 8. Remington double barrel rifle; 9. Meriden loading tube in stock about 1870; 10. Old peep sight cap & ball rifle; 11. Kentucky rifle; 12. (lying down) unidentified; 13. Civil War Confederate saber from Shiloh hill; 14. Assortment of powder and shot holders. —*Courtesy Sam Houston Museum, Huntsville, Texas. Reproduced by Revelle Studio, Huntsville.*

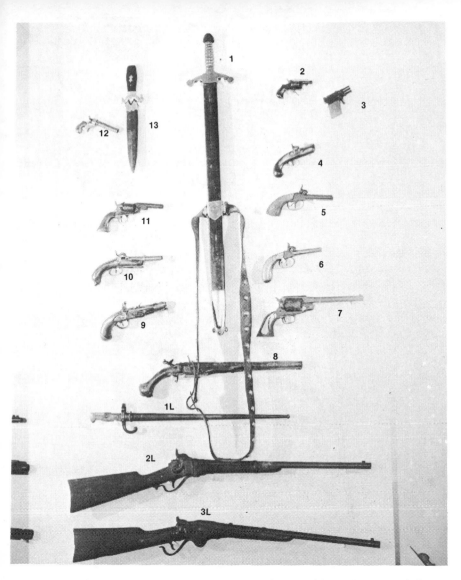

PART of gun collection—Clockwise, beginning with Saber—1. Civil War sword; 2. French pocket pistol; 3. German EMGE; 4. Spanish derringer; 5. American made cap & ball 46 caliber; 6. English single shot; 7. Remington 1858; 8. Mediterranean flintlock pistol; 9. French military flintlock pistol; 10. Sidearm used in Civil War; 11. Possibly early Colt baby dragoon; 12. unidentified; 13. Knife for throwing; Lower Part—1. Bayonet, Civil War period; 2. Sharps rifle; 3. Breechloading cap & ball rifle. —*Courtesy of Sam Houston Museum, Huntsville, Texas.*

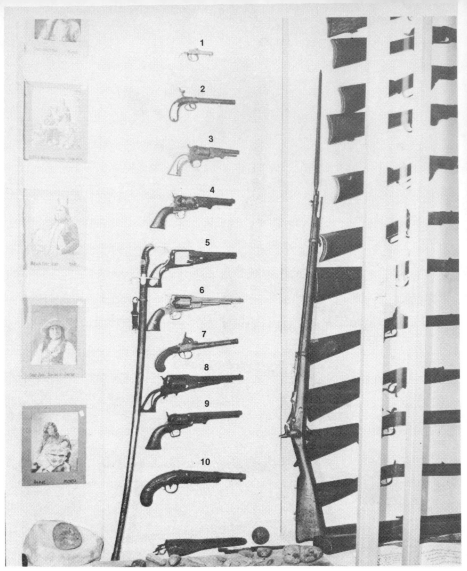

PART of gun collection with Indian photos; Indians, top to bottom,
Little Wound, Ogalala; Bear Foot Chief, Brule; Chief Josh, San Carlos
Apache; Ah-a-he, Wichita; grinding stone. Guns, top to bottom; 1.
Old bronze English pistol; 2. Single barrel piston of 1880; 3. Muzzle
loading cap & ball; 4. Cylinder, shot cap & ball; 5. Old gun found on
battlefield at Sashita; 6. Cap & ball six-shooter; 7. Cap & ball muzzle
loader 1840; 8. Cap & ball Remington six-shooter 1858; 9. Cap & ball
six-shooter silver cavalry gun; 10. Cap & ball muzzle loader ''Savage''
1850; Standing U.S. bayonet, used at San Juan Hill; Lower, assortment of arrow heads and grinding stones. —*Courtesy Sam Houston
Museum, Huntsville, Texas.*

APPENDIX A

When he was only nineteen years of age, Temple Lea Houston was chosen to give an address at the San Jacinto Battlefield. He was already well known (among friends at college and business associates of his father) as a speaker who could captivate and hold the attention of his audience. He was also the son of the hero of the Battle of San Jacinto, who won Texas her Independence from Mexico.

ADDRESS OF TEMPLE LEA HOUSTON, SAN JACINTO BATTLEFIELD, WEDNESDAY, APRIL 21, 1880

While their patriotism is in its full strength, it is a custom among all nations to celebrate the anniversaries of the great events of their history. The observance of this custom evinces national vitality; its neglect evinces a decrease of that spirit which is the strongest bulwark of a people's liberty. It thrills my heart with pride when I look around me now and see that grand old Washington, the queen county of the state, can gather within her fertile bosom an audience like this who, by their presence here today, show that they are not unmindful of the heroes who shed their blood on our early battlefields that we might be free. Only patriots honor their patriotic dead; and, while this reverence for the great dead exists among our people, the flames on the altars of Texas liberty will never cease to burn.

In the brief remarks I make, beyond a few necessary allusions, I treat the battle, of which today is the anniversary, simply as a link through the brightest of the shining chain of events which compose the history of Texas. In the early morning of this

85

century the great Southwest slept in the unbroken stillness of barbarism. The immense territories between the Mississippi and the Pacific Ocean, between the Rio Grande and the British possession, were an almost unpeopled waste and knew no lord save the plumed and quivered Algonquin. Texas was then a grand wilderness and, except for a few widely distant missions planted by the heroic Catholics, was solely beneath the dominion of the savage. Then these same breezes, with their airy wings laden with perfume stolen from the flowers, swept over these broad plains, but fanned not the cheek of the Anglo-Saxon. These same streams, rolling on toward the ocean to mingle their crystal waters with her stormy surges, murmured as sweetly and sparkled as brightly as now but moistened not the lips of civilized man, neither did they kiss the prow of a steamer or turn a single mill-wheel. The brown buffalo cropped undisturbed the green grass from yonder prairie, and the spotted deer rested unfrightened beneath the cool shade of these forest monarchs.

But this scene was destined soon to change. On the mountains of Virginia was born a man on whose brow was stamped the seal of genius and whose young but great heart was fired with the inspiration of a high and holy purpose. That man was Stephen F. Austin. It was his hand that rent the veil of mystery that had shrouded Texas and turned thither-ward the tide of emigration, thus mingling the waves of two civilizations, from the conflict of which have followed such incalculable effect on the history of this continent. Against the spotless name of Austin calumny has breathed no stain. His lofty nature stood unmoved alike amid the threats of male-clad hand of power, the horrors of a Mexican dungeon, and the splendid offers of princely wealth. The brevity of my time bids me leave him, but I could not pass in the presence of such a name without paying a humble tribute to its greatness and purity. This broad state is his monument, and his epitaph is written in the hearts of these people who can so justly call him father.

We, today, dwell upon the third act in the drama of American freedom. The first was to strike from the limbs of the thirteen colonies the shackles of British tyranny; the second was to wrench from the dark grasp of the savage territories between the Mississippi and the Alleghanies; the third, the grandest, was to wrest from the mitre of the bigot and the sceptre of the despot, the imperial domains ceded by Mexico to the United States. It is only given the speaker to notice the third.

At the commencement of her revolution, the population of Texas only reached 30,000 but scattered over a wide space of country. The causes that led to this revolt are too well known to here need notice. The decisive campaign was ominous to the cause of freedom. The Alamo, after an immortal resistance, fell without a savior among her defenders. This tremendous disaster was followed by the defeat of Fannin at Coleto, Goliad, accompanied by the appalling massacre of the captured. Then the invader, with his red hand warm and dripping with the blood of murdered innocence, marched his columns for the Brazos. His plan was simply completed and revealed the hand of a master.

The first division was to reach Nacogdoches via Bastrop and Washington. The route of the second lay along the coast from Victoria to Anahuac, embracing Brazoria and Galveston. The third and central division under Santa Anna was to rejoin the second at Anahuac, first passing through Columbus, San Felipe, and Harrisburg. The Texas army retreated steadily from Gonzales to the Brazos, and was kept there for some time for two reasons; First, the troops were disheartened by the recent heavy reverses; and, therefore, unfit to meet the enemy; Second, a laxity of discipline had ensued which it was necessary to correct and enforce and correct with proper obedience. These purposes being gained, the Texas army marched down the left bank of the Brazos, the Mexican army crossing that stream at Richmond.

On April 21st, 1836, forty-four years ago today, the two armies met at San Jacinto, between Anahuac and Lynchburg. The action was begun at 3 P.M. by the Texas cavalry. A general movement followed along the whole line, but the engagement lasted but eighteen minutes. But Texan vengeance, roused by the massacres of Alamo and Goliad, was not sated until the shades of night had darkened the face of the earth. Grand beyond the power of words, beyond the reach of imagination, have been the results of this battle on the history, geography, the commerce of this continent. The almost immediate effects of the battle of San Jacinto brought on the war between the United States and Mexico, resulting in an immense accession of territory to the United States; so that, under the influence of this battle, the boundaries of the United States leaped from the Mississippi to the Pacific, and her limits spread until they reached from the sandy wastes of Sonora to the dark regions of the North "where rolls the Oregon, and hears no sound save his own dashings."

Since these vast realms have come beneath the sway of the Anglo-Saxon, the plastic hand of civilization has wrought many changes in their primeval magnificence. Had it not been for the Battle of San Jacinto, the tide of emigration would not yet have reared opulent cities in the far west. The majestic silence of the Rocky Mountains would be a stranger to the shriek of the locomotive, and their awful solitudes would be broken by no sound save the deep roar of their swollen torrents as they leap down their black chasms, and the tremendous crash of their falling ice fields as they leap from their frozen homes, desolating the green valleys nestling far beneath. The golden wealth of California would still sleep in the bosom of her mountain gorges, and the silver treasures of Nevada would yet slumber in their caverned homes.

And, where the Texas veterans—the brave men who set these giant causes in motion? But few are left among us now; and each year that passes thins their ranks. The scythe of death has been mowing fast among them. The few that are with us view a spectacle like of which meets no other eyes on earth. On whatsoever side they turn, their venerable gaze rests upon naught but the reverence and gratitude felt for them by the people of this state. They look down upon a broad empire which they have conquered from the Aztec and the Comanche. These old men are grey with years; their hair has whitened in the conflicts of their country; and around their aged temples is bound a patriot's wreath woven by hands that are free and tied by fingers that are free, more glorious by far than the most resplendent diadem that ever glittered upon the brow of royalty. While they are among us, we can bow in reverence to them; and, when they leave us, mourn their departure and hope that their warrior souls are wafted to another land by the side of whose brightness the splendors of day are dim, a land where the vollied thunders of musketry are silent, where the cannon's deepening roar has no echo, a land where the sound of battle never comes, where the tread of armies not heard.

One more word, and I am finished. May my eyes never view a divided Texas! The voice of division is already heard in some parts of the state. If we were to divide this sacred heritage left us by our fathers, to whom would you give her national history? —for she has one. To what torn section would you give her battlefields around which cluster so many glorious memories? To what rent portion would you give the old capitol that sits upon the hill at Austin? To what broken fragment of lovely Texas would you give the banner with the "lone star," the blue field and three stripes? To whom, the memory of her dead heroes, orators, and statesmen! To whom the band of old war-scarred veterans that still linger among us as if they stayed but to watch over the unity of the state they won from the Mexican and Indian?

If Texas will only preserve her unity, she can wield controlling influence in national affairs. Immigration is constantly streaming in our borders; and in a few years, when the waste places are made to smile, when lowing herds feed on all our plains, when all our prairies are covered with the golden treasures of the wheat harvest and the green splendor of the corn field, when all our glad valleys glisten in the white wealth of the cotton crop, when Texas attains her full growth, her voice when spoken in the halls of Congress will echo all over the land and sway the councils of the nation.

The interest of our state enjoins unity upon her children. Nations like individuals carry within themselves the seeds of their future dissolution. The germs of death already lurk in the vitals of the American Republic. The same fatal influences that have wrought the downfall of other republics have begun to sap the lifeblood of our own. I say, with sadness, that history records no instance where a republic registered the silent workings of the frightful causes that now begin to permeat every vein and artery of the American Republic. Of late years there has been a fearful deterioration of morals. Priestly robes and judicial ermine have, alike, caught the infection. Corruption has sullied the purity of the high places. Courts and Congresses have been bought and sold like merchandise; bayonets have gleamed the senate halls; and the most hallowed precedents of the past have been violated and ruthlessly trampled upon. A few colossal and soulless corporations of fabuless (*sic.*) wealth wrung from the masses, are in league with those in power to wrest the last vestige of freedom from the people of this land. The vast system of railroads, spreading over the continent in every direction, are theirs; the white-winged fleets of trade that ride the billows of the ocean are subject to the same sceptre—the gold mines, the silver belts, the coal fields, the vast lumber forests, the cotton market, the wheat regions bow to the same supremacy—all hostile to our liberty.

All these signs are fraught with deep meaning and, in tones not to be mistaken, tell us that the outlook is storm-cast and threatening. And, that is why Texas should preserve her unity. For with all the might and attributes, the population and extent of a great nation, she can safely enjoy all the benefits and avoid the evils resulting from her connection with the American Union and smile at the dangers that would crush and crumble weaker states. And, when our sister states are wrecked by their own dissensions or crushed beneath the iron heel of despotism, Texas can lift proudly her stromless crest and gather from the ruins of the now tottering edifice of the American Union a new and safer structure and be the isthmus over which shall pass to future ages and the dearest boon of man—political freedom. When these considerations occur, where is the fractricidal hand that would twice tear in twain the glorious fabric reared by the Austins, Wharton, Rusk, and others not less noted, that was cemented by the blood of Bowie, Fannin, Crockett, and Travis.

No man with a patriot's heart or a statesman's head would wish to see Texas dragged down from the eminence of an empire to the low level of a few petty, ignoble, dishonored states.

Despite its youth, this state has a glorious history filled with stirring events and splendid achievements. For her, with a sparse population, to win her independence from a powerful oppressor and drive the Indian from her borders, requires heroism equal to any displayed by the soldiers of Salamis and Platea. The blood of Texas is sprinkled over this continent from the blue heights of Gettysburg to the palace halls of the Montezumas. And, of all that blood not one drop was shed in an unjust cause; on no battlefield have her children ever shown less courage than that of him, who from the beleaguered wall of the Alamo, said "I will never surrender." With ancestors and a history such as we have, it matters not what may happen to the nations around us—it matters not what doom may overtake the Union or how many stars are stricken from the constellation of American states—I fondly believe that our Texas will never part with one of her rights. For our countrymen freedom can never meet her death in the land where an Alamo was her birth place, and liberty can never find her grave where the ashes of Travis sleep.

References

Sam Houston Museum, Huntsville, Texas; files on Temple Lea Houston.

APPENDIX B

DEFENCE OF GEN. HOUSTON

The following was received by Temple Houston in response to a letter he had written in connection with his research into the statements in H.S. Thrall's *History of Texas* that in some instances slandered General Sam Houston. Temple wanted to clarify the facts before he spoke out in rebuke of Thrall.

Baylor University
Independence, Texas
November 4th, 1880

My Esteemed Young Friend:

Your note of 1st is before me. In the book of Records, referred to by Rev. H.S. Thrall, as being in my possession, written in the handwriting of W.D. Miller, Esq., and signed by Sam Houston; *I have never seen any letter of instructions,* to Jacob Snively. —A copy of a letter appointing him (Jacob Snively) an Inspector General: —and a speech of Gen. Houston, when U.S. Senator, delivered in the U.S. Senate, making the admission that the Snively Expedition was authorized are herewith enclosed.

Your Sincere Friend,
Wm. Carey Crane.

The passage relative to the Snively Expedition in the speech alluded to by Dr. Crane (delivered August 1, 1854) reads as follows:

The Expedition under Colonel Snively had been ordered to intercept, if possible, a convoy from St. Louis to Santa Fe. That does not look much like a denial! It would be quite singular if Houston would one moment admit the legality of the Expedition, and on the same floor, and before the same men deny the truth of the words he uttered. Such conduct would present a parallel to Mr. Thrall, when he says Fannin did, and did not receive orders.

Either the failure to find the denial, or to produce the letter of instructions, would brand Thrall and his partners in Calumy with the disgrace which they conspired to inflict upon another; but it seems that they confined neither the denial nor the letter! Mr. Thrall virtually surrenders the fight, and says that this villianous (*sic.*) accusation is made on the authority so stated of H.F. Young! Surely Mr. Thrall should not have charged Houston with an offense having all the moral essentials of perjury merely on hearsay. He should have reflected that in case he fails to substantiate a charge of such gravity, that the odium which he seeks to fasten upon another recoils upon himself. If this did not occur to him, he realizes it now. It is the very worst class of criminals that turn states-evidence, this Mr. Thrall has done. He lays his own blunders upon his printers, charges his absurd and false representations of Texas scenes upon his publishers and now tries to make his friends bear the weight of his refuted slanders. He openly acknowledges that Young is his only authority for this awful charge. I never heard of Young until I saw his name linked with Thralls in an attempt to villify a dead man. Thrall calls him "Col." Young. I do not know where he got the commission or to what brigade his regiment was attached; but suppose every man in that regiment was killed as saving the gallant "Colonel." I know no living man that belonged to it. But if he is a man of character, why does he rest silent under the imputations borne by my words, for I denounced a statement for which his name is authority, as false. If he wishes his sanction to add any strength to a statement he had best rescue his name from the stain cast upon it, not by my words alone—but by the absence of facts, for the existence of which his name is invoked as security. The fiend who at midnight stealthily enters a room, and buries his murderous steel in the breast of a sleeping enemy, is utterly abhorrent—but speech has no power to tell the baseness of the cowardly wretch who assassinates character—when too, its wearer has long since mouldered into helpless dust. In my words I include one and all who authorized these Calumnies which Thrall so willingly circulated. For it is a fact not hidden from me, that this pliant minion of malice, Thrall, preferred these charges at the instance of Houston enemies. He made these accusations under a warranty for their truth, and now he finds that the warranty is as worthless as the title which it purported to secure. This rusty blunderbuss (his History) was loaded up with falsehoods and calumnies, and fired at Houston's memory: the charge missed its aim, but the recoil prostrated the miserable, deluded creature who pulled the trigger. Not long since a person over the signature of "E" attacked my first article. He did not sign his name, but crawled and coiled up behind the little letter "E," and safe in his obscurity struck at me. He was concealed and sheltered behind that little letter—and the same small space will amply hide millions of such infinitesimal insects. When one writes publicly, attacking or defending another, they should sign their name, but I presume that "E" knowing full well that his support would damage Mr. Thrall, wisely concealed his identity. I would have written my review sooner, but only learned of these slanders last April, and was withheld some time by those around me, who said that it would seem more appropriate for Houston's friends, rather than one of his sons to vindicate him. It is said that my words are too bitter. I ask any one to read Thrall's charges and place themselves in my position, and I feel that they will not renew the complaint. The frigid villiany (*sic.*), with which he renews a charge, proven to be false, is an eloquent apology for any degree of bitterness. I am aware that in writing these articles I have made enemies but I cannot regret it, when, I reflect that I made them in defending the truth of Texas history, and in resenting an insult to the intelligence of my countrymen; In making these attacks I have lost friends, but the good name of a father should be more to a son, than the friendship of any man or set of men.

Temple Houston

Georgetown, November 7, 1880

References

Sam Houston Museum, Huntsville, Texas; Files on Temple Lea Houston.

APPENDIX C

Another article was written by Temple Houston in an effort to clear the name of his father from statements made in Homer S. Thrall's *Pictorial History of Texas*. In this article he calls attention to several passages and some pictures he considered to be erroneous. He mentions Thrall's uncalled for omissions. In several accounts, names of people important to the history of Texas were omitted, according to Houston.

Here again is an example of the tenderness and high regard in which he held his fathers memory. It is a glorious tribute to a man well known to history, General Sam Houston, given by a son who could hardly remember him.

THRALL'S HISTORY OF TEXAS

In your issue of October 15th, was a sickly communication from Rev. H.S. Thrall, which I would only treat with the silence of contempt, were it not that it contains a reiteration of a charge, which it is incumbent on me to refute, and while doing so, I shall notice other features of his article and make a few observations on his "History"—but there are many things in his "History" which I shall not now notice such as the I. and G.N.R.R. bridge across the Colorado at Austin, and the cross-eyed picture of the "old alcalde" —(p. 843) when his excellency was not cross-eyed. He says, that these are typographical errors in his "History." True, but that was not charged in my review; neither did I accuse his history of any faults that can be vallidated on such grounds. Whenever I made a charge I quoted his exact words, or cited the page and in every instance his language was capable of but one construction, and its meaning too plain to be distorted by any typographical errors. So the object of his admission is unknown unless to assume a mask of candor, which the features of slander will never wear with ease. I would here lay down the broad premise, that an author is responsible for the contents of his book, especially after he has seen the first copy, and permits others like it to be published, and reaps profits from the same. In my former article were cited four illustrations which were gross misrepresentations of the largest rivers of Texas, and the character, and size of rivers, are an index to the territories watered by them. Now, Mr. Thrall saddles the guilt of these fraudelent illustrations, published, and sanctioned the fraud by his silence! If the fraud was not of his approval, why did he not stop it? Why did he permit six editions of his work to come out, each containing what he knew was a fraud? His effort to place the guilt upon the publishers is the wretched artifice of low cunning—the miserable device of a detested imposter to atone for the deception which he sought to practice. There is guilt somewhere, and if Thrall reaped the profits of it, he must share the odium. His apology for the omission of Judge Wheeler's name is equally pitiable, and even if true, could not Wheeler's name have been inserted in a later edition? For as even little ''E'' says the work has been out eighteen months! It must be a hard matter to get pictures of four rivers of Texas, and to gather facts about the lives of her Chief Justice! It would be an easy matter to get pictures of those streams, and substitute them for the present absurd representations. And if Mr. Thrall will only look in the first part of the 27th Texas Reports, he will find a beautiful biography of Judge Wheeler, written by the fluent pen of Major C.S. West, who, as a man and a lawyer, stands unrivaled in Texas. And since almost every illustration in ''Baker's Texas Scrap Book'' is appropriated by Mr. Thrall, he might have consulted the Biography of Wheeler found in that well written book without which no Texas library is complete.

Suppose we admit the sincerity of his apology for the slight offered Wheeler's memory. It does not excuse the ommission of James Willis and of Jones Reves and of other enumerated in my former article. In his biographical sketches Mr. Thrall should have noticed that heroic South Carolinian, Bonham, who fell at the Alamo, and whose name is graven on one of the four sides of the monument in the Capital Gallery in Austin—the other three sides bearing the names, Bowie, Crockett and Travis. He simply has no excuse, and offers none: but in failing to do so, shows more judgment than when making his miserable explanation of his misrepresentation of Texas Scenery, and of the absence of Wheeler's name. Neither does he deny his intention to reflect on Yoakum, (while quoting so profusely from him). Suppose the Hall he names was W.D.C. Hall, it does not follow that he is more credible than Capt. McKim, or as much so, as to make a conflict between their statements the basis of a reflection on Yoakum's authenticity. Mr. Thrall in no wise accounts for his direct contradiction of himself when he says, Fannin did receive orders (p. 251) and that he did not receive them (p. 248) and (p. 259). When I charge Mr. Thrall with handling the truth with penurious frugality, I am kind enough to point to the page and I insist that he return the compliment, and point to the page of the Senate Journals, and find Houston's device of legal character of the Snively Expedition, and also produce the letter of instructions. He also denies us the benefit of his idea on cannibalism, which (from his expression on page 445) I was exceedingly anxious to learn. Neither does he deny charges of plagiarism, because if he does I will fasten his guilt upon him with evidence direct and conclusive. He will not dare deny the charge. His silence under this will be accepted as a plea of guilty, so I insist if he is innocent that he give his friends the benefit of his denial even if he is indifferent to his own reputation.

In regard to his insinuation about Burnet, Sidney Sherman, the Jacks and Wharton and Lemar being Sam Houston's enemies, I have only to say that these facts are history, and to intimate ignorance of them ill becomes a man who presumes to write a History of Texas. These enmities are facts and I have no wish that they, or their causes, should be hidden from the "young men of Texas." Thrall betrays an ignorance of these things, and as much as intimates that, even if they are facts, they will not be found in his "History"—thus plainly showing, that he would not pause to conceal or distort the truth! And yet, young men of Texas, such a character as this has dared to write what he pompously styles a "History of our State." While through friendship (?) for Houston he would not hesitate to suppress his public enmities, he does not scruple to charge him with uttering a monstrous falsehood! Consistent indeed! But Thrall in failing to prove this charge, becomes shrouded in the deep infamy with which he sought to darken anothers name. I would a thousand times rather have said it, that any men were Houston's enemies, than that such as Thrall were his friends; and when he numbers himself among Houston's friends, he attempts to cast another foul aspersion upon Houston's name "the most unkindest cut of all." His work is no "History," for it does not give the heroic women of Texas the glory due them. Of all those who came out here in the early times—in the days the Mexican and of the Indian—and shared the toils and dangers of the fathers of Texas—and without whom there would have been no Texas—not one is given a place among the "Distinguished" of our State! He might at least have given some space to Mrs. Mary Bell, the heroine of Austin's colony, and mother of Judge James H. Bell,—to Mrs. Sarah A., the wife of William H. Wharton, to Mrs. Moverick—to Mrs. Jno. Brown, the mother of Hon. Jno. Henry Brown—to Mrs. Broches of Gonzales,—to Mrs. Francis Sutherland of Jackson County,—to Mrs. Jno. J. Linn of Victoria—such names as these—the mothers of Texas—should be chiseled in marble—they may sound strange to some ears—but in the minds of the old Texans—those that were christened in the fires of the early battles—they make memories stirring and glorious, with which these pure, bright, heroic names are linked forever. No history of a land can be written, that denies glory to the mothers of that land, and the absence of names like the above, forms a chasm in Mr. Thrall's work, for which there can be no palliation. In my former article, I alluded to a passage in the "History" (p. 335) where Mr. Thrall said that he had seen a letter of Sam Houston's instructing Snively to undertake an expedition, the legal character of which expedition Houston denied in the U.S. Senate. I asked Mr. Thrall to point to the page of the Journal of the Senate that contained Houston's denial of the legality of the expedition, and to have the letter of instructions identified by certain men whose reputations are statewide. Instead of meeting the issue as presented, he quails like a sentenced felon. He does not name the page, but only says the denial is found in the debates of the U.S. Senate, well knowing that the deliberations of that body cover a period of almost one hundred years! I insist that he find his denial, or retract the statement. He says that the letter of instructions is in the Book of Records, in the handwriting of W.D. Miller in the possession of Dr. Crane—each letter signed "Sam Houston." The following certificate shows the fallacy of that statement:

(The certificate from Dr. Wm. Carey Crane was shown at the beginning of Chapter two to show that Temple Houston had checked the records and was correct in his accusations of Mr. Thrall.)

References

Amarillo Sunday Globe News, Library.

APPENDIX D

After his address at the San Jacinto Battle anniversary a year and a half earlier, Houston was invited to dedicate the Monument.

HOUSTON'S EULOGY TO TEXAS HEROES
Delivered at the unveiling of the Monument to Heroes of San Jacinto, at Galveston, Texas.
August 25, 1881

I would wish my auditors to understand that I attribute the honor of this invitation, not to my personal importance, but to the fact that I happen to be the child of one of the soldiers of San Jacinto. The pleasure that I derive from this occasion is lessened by the absence of Mollie E. Moore Davis. Could I have stood beside her tonight, I would have felt more than honored, for I know that I speak the voice of my State when I say that hers is as sweet a tongue as ever rung the silver chimes of earthly thought.

It is a beautiful custom to free people to rear above the last resting places of their heroic dead, some token commemorative of the cause in which they fell, and expressive of the grateful reverence felt toward them by posterity. This gratitude dwells in the breast of freedom only—no real hero's monument was ever built by a race of slaves. The decay of monuments, the forgetfulness of departed greatness, are sure procursors of a nations fall. It is with a proud consciousness that I view the sea-girt city, the island queen, first in honoring the memory of our dead heroes, as she is first in population and commercial greatness, wearing with the jewels of her wealth a patriotism that seems all the brighter for adorning the metropolis of the southwest.

While, this patriotic reverence dwells in the hearts of our people, the flames on the altars of Texas liberty will never cease to burn. On an occasion like this one realizes the feebleness of language; it speaks so little of what is felt. The story of the strife in which our heroes fell need not be told; history recorded it. Their valor needs no eulogy, even could my lowly lips utter such. For Fame's clarion has sounded their praises, and earth is the only limit of their renown. But as in the sheer magnitude of its results, the battle of San Jacinto has but few, if any, parallels, allusion to those results may not seem improper. Never before has the surface of a land changed with such marvelous rapidity as has Texas in the last four or five decades. Only a few years back and the plumed and crested Alongonquin roamed over magnificient Texas, sole lord of its vast wastes, save where a few isolated missions sought vainly to weave religion's silken fetters over the savage mind. Yonder billows, blue and restless, dashed then as grandly against your level shores as now, but on their tossing bosoms floated not the freighted wealth of earth's nations as does now. These same breezes, damp from dalliance with the waves, and laden with perfume stolen from the flowers swept over our broad plains, but fanned not the cheek of civilized man. Our silver streams, rolling on to mingle their crystal waters with the stormy surges of the great deep, murmured as sweetly and sparkled as brightly as now, but they moistened not the lips of the Anglo-Saxon and turned not a single mill wheel, nor cotton nor wheat field smiled in all their valleys. The brown buffalo cropt undisturbed, the green grass from our prairies, and the spotted deer rested unfrightened beneath the cool shade of our forest oaks. Texas, lovely Texas was as fair, as fresh, and as beautiful as was Eden when God, delighted, gazed on the new-born world. It was thus when came the men whose memory we to-day honor.

These pioneers were the heralds of a new civilization—one that was born in the medieval convulsions of England, nurtured under the shadow of Virginia's Mountains, and flashed forth freed and panoplied from the struggles of the American revolution—a civilization whose fundamental principle was civil and religious liberty. Coming to Texas, it rested for a moment under the frown of the Spanish civilization, which was developed on the glittering thrones of Europe, and in the torture chambers of the Inquisition. One idolized, the other abhorred civil and religious liberty. When the Anglo-Saxon settlements had attained a magnitude sufficient to invite governmental interference, the Mexicans adopted toward them an oppressive policy, typical of their institutions. This ignited the spark. You know the result; to-day is celebrative of those who suffered to bring them about. The conflict of the opposite types of civilization for the mastery of this continent was decided on the forest fringed banks of a Texas stream. Never before in the history of the world were such gigantic results intrusted to so few combatants; but here let me say, sterner warriors or truer patriots than those who guarded the liberty of Texas, on that imortal day, never trod a battle-field. Had that little band quailed before the might of invading despotism, our Pacific shores might yet be unknown; The golden wealth of California would yet sleep in her mountain gorges; the silver treasures of Nevada would now slumber, hidden in their caverned home; the two oceans would not have shaken hands across the completed lines of railways; the solitude of the Rocky Mountains would yet be a stranger to the shriek of the locomotive, and their awful silence broken by no sound save the voice of nature, when spoken in the deep roar of her swollen cataracts, in the rolling peals of her warring storms, and in the tremendous crash of her falling ice-fields, as they lept from their frozen homes, and desolate the green valleys meeting her beneath. On earth there walk no men like the veterans who freed Texas. Only a few of them linger among us now, and they will be here but a little while longer. Each year that passes thins their ranks. A few more days and the last will be gone. One by one the pale messenger is calling them across that river whose viewless farther shore is wrapt in the mists of doubt, the clouds of death. They hear another reveille whose floating notes we cannot catch. Are they gathering for a grander battle? While they are among us we feel toward them with a devotion whose depth speech can never tell. No minions cringe around them, no servile lance is bent to them, but the homage of a free nation is more than royal offering laid before them. No ducal star glitters on their breasts, no shining coronet encircles their brows, but around their gray locks beams a glory, by the side of which kingly splendors are dim. Cling tenderly to these old men, for when they are gone nothing like them is left. Strike down your men of eminence, to-day, these who fill your highest seats, and with a wave of your hand you can summon around you hundreds like them—for the gifted sons of Texas are many—but when one of these old warriors drops from the line, earth has none to fill his place. Bitterly do we know that they leave us forever, for of all the manly forms laid low beneath the rod of death, none have ever risen; of all the bright eyes he has closed, none have ever looked their loveliness on earth again; of all the eloquent lips silenced by His hand, none have ever spoken again; of all the noble hearts whose warm beatings have been stilled by his chilling touch, none ever throbbed on earth again.

The fathers of Texas have left her in the hands of another generation. Is it worthy of the trust? I believe it is. As yet the burden weighs but lightly. But with the swift footsteps of the future there is coming an hour when banded gold, soulless wealth, will oppress the lowlier classes,—an event that marks an era in every republic, when leagued capital, not claiming worth or services as its right to sway, but wielding as its scepter only so much yellow dust, seeks to force men to bow to its ignoble supremacy. It is where power passes from the cottage to the palace. History tells not where a republic resisted this fatal influence. In our Republic's life that period is not a great way off. And in that hour Texas will need men—I am speaking now to the young man—to the bright-eyed boys of Texas. In that hour your State will need men, not, oh! not, the paid politicians of the present, who seek office for its gold, not its glory; who trade in honor and traffic in eminence! But she will need statesmen in her councils and warriors on her battle-fields. She will want the mighty intellect, the grand in soul; more than that—the pure in heart. Do you want an example? Look at yon Texas veterans! The mould in which the great are cast is yet unbroken. Let your patriotism be like that of the young Irishman serving in England's armies, who was mortally shot in the breast on a battle-field in Spain. He knew that he would die. While his lifeblood ebbed fast away, he thought of the green fields of his country, his cottage home, of the little fire-side group there that he would see never more, and while the hot tears ran down his boyish cheeks he seized a goblet, and holding it under his red and gushing wound until it filled with his bright blood, he lifted it on high, watched it glitter a moment in the sunlight, and casting it on the earth, he exclaimed: ''Oh, Erin! my country! would to God that was shed for you!'' I believe in my heart that the young men of Texas are worthy of the glorious burden borne by them. Listen not to the serpent hiss of him who would counsel State or National division. He that would wish to dim and divide the splendor of the Lone Star's beams is as little a patriot as one who would seek to shatter the constellation of which Texas is the brightest number. Revere the memory of your forefathers, follow their examples, obey their teachings, and then the deeds commemorated by that moment have not been performed in vain, and the hallowed soil on which it rests will be free forever.

References:

Sam Houston Museum, Files on Temple Houston, Huntsville, Texas

APPENDIX E

Following is a letter from R.M. Hall to Temple Lea Houston while Hall was living in Austin and Houston was living in Mobeetie. In later years in Woodward, Oklahoma, the two men became partners.

Austin, Texas, Oct. 23rd, 1887

Hon. Temple Houston
Mobeetie, Texas,

My Dear Sir:

Your highly appreciated favor of the 18th Inst reached me yesterday. Although much pressed for time, I shall endeaver to answer your inquiries, and respond fittingly to the hopes and sentiments you express. Hopes that the effect of the new land law now beginning to be felt in the North West, may be to develope and populate your section and advance the prosperity of the whole state: to increase the loyalty of your people to Texas, and their respect for her laws; and not to beget a feeling that Texas is unkind or unjust to any of her citizens; or that her laws are unequal or partial. Your sentiments of personal regards, and confidence in my honesty of purpose to carry out this law without fear or favor, to the best of my ability, is very gratifying to me, coming from your neighborhood: and particularly so, coming from you. Your zeal for the developement of the Panhandle, and your solicitude for the boni fide settler, as the chief instrument for that work has not diminished, I perceive, since you were here as Senator last Winter. From our intimate intercourse then, and from your labors here, I know how genuine was this solicitude. Hence the anxiety you now express that the settler be assured that his rights cannot be interfered with, or curtailed, secures my sympathy and quick response.

I am confident that a few more weeks time will demonstrate to every settler that his every right under the law is safe, and no one will dare question or interfere with a single one of them. It is unnecessary to quote the law to you, you are perfectly familiar with ever provision of it. You are aware that the essence of it, the prime feature of it are first, to hold the public lands for, and sell them to actual settlers only: second, to stop the free use and occupancy of these lands, and to utilize them for the benefit of the funds to which they belong: in otherwords, for the benefit of the whole people. The cotton pickers of central and east Texas have just as much interest in these lands as the people of the west. This law gives every actual settler who was on any of these lands when the law took effect. Six months from the time said lands are classified in which to make application to purchase. Very few settlers are ignorant, I feel sure, of this provision.

Of the thirty million acres of land still belonging to the State, about five million acres have been leased. The leases cover lands which were supposed, from the information possessed at the time said leases were executed, not to be in demand for immediate settlement.

The rules and regulations which have been adopted as provided by this law, give every settler who was on any leased land at the time said lease was filed for record in the county clerks office, six months from the date said lands are put upon the market for sale, in which to make his application for purchase. Thus you see any settler who may happen to be upon a given section when it is leased, can remain there until six months after an opportunity is given him to purchase. If any lessee in the Panhandle has been so ignorant of the law as to order a settler to leave, whose right to remain is so amply secured and fortified, his ignorance should almost excuse him. He will certainly be enlightened before the settler goes. I am surprised to learn from you that the settlers in the lease of the 'Rocking Chair Ranch' are really disturbed by the order of the Manager of the company to leave. The communication to the Governor, dated Mobeetie, October 6th, and signed by Wm. Jones and G.W. Boyd; purporting to represent about thirty families who are settled in the range of the 'Rocking Chair Ranch' Company in Collingsworth County, was refered to me by the Governor.

In response thereto, I have directed an Agent of the State to proceed to that locality, and report in full all the facts of the case. While there, he will classify the lands occupied by the settlers, who may then purchase whenever they please within the next six months.

None of these settlers have ever written to the General Land Office to inform the department of their presence there, or to invite attention to their wants and interests. And when I noticed that said communication was in the hand writing of Hon. J.N. Browning, and that it also appeared promptly in his personal organ and was made a text by the antilease, free grass press of the State which endeavored to persuade the public that Scotch Syndicates were evicting settlers from their homes; I suspected that perhaps Messrs James and Boyd were being used as tools.

This said communication was altogether premature, for at the time it was written the 'Rocking Chair' Company had no lease, nor is their lease in force at this moment, for it was not delivered by me until yesterday; hence has not yet been filed for record. The manager who ordered the settlers to leave several weeks ago, was so absurdly previous that he must have intended to perpetrate a joke.

The application for this lease was made on the ninth day of July last. The lease was awarded on the fifteenth day of July.

When I was in Mobeetie in August I met a settler from this 'Rocking Chair' range; he did not inform me what sections he was occupying but complained of the lease in question. In answer to my inquiries as to why he did not apply to lease land enough to provide for the cattle he owned, (about a hundred head I think), he replied that he had 'not made up his mind' what he wanted to do. He was then told that the 'Rocking

Chair' Ranch Company had not paid the money on their lease when I left the office, and that the lands in question were open to other applicants.

About a month after this, Mr. Jones, another settler, seems to have made up his mind what to do, for on the 23rd day of Sept. he filed his application to lease three sections, which were awarded to him notwithstanding they had previously been awarded as above mentioned. Subsequently, the Rocking Chair Ranch Co. paid the amount due on their award, and a lease was executed; which lease was held up however, and was not delivered until yesterday, in the hope that Mr. Jones would consummate his lease thus giving one the same courtesy and indulgence as the other.

Up to this date Mr. Jones has not paid, nor has he made any excuse; but instead, he has signed a letter (written by Mr. Browning) to the Governor. If Messrs Jones and Boyd are responsible for this letter, they know the rights of settlers under this law too well, to have been disturbed by an order to leave by the manager of the syndicate of *any nationality,* they know also, that when this law speaks of settlers, it does not allude to cattle. They know also that any man who has a hundred cattle, or a hundred thousand, and expects to graze them upon school lands, in whole or in part, must make a contract with the State or else he is in daily risk of being disturbed by some-one who does make such a contract; or if he undertakes to appropriate one section of this land, or a thousand sections, contrary to law, and without such a contract, the State will disturb him as soon as the State is informed.

I repeat the Settlers in the Rocking Chair pasture are safe; but if they fail or refuse to provide for their cattle it is their own fault.

Every settler on the agricultural section can purchase said section, and keep within said pasture sixty four head of cattle. Every settler on a grazing section can purchase said section, and three others, and turn loose two hundred and fifty six head. It is now too late for them to lease, although they have had ample time to do so. If they fail to or refuse to purchase within six months after classification, they will be trespassers, and the lands they are on will be for sale to another purchaser.

No, the cattlemen of the Panhandle large and small alike have heretofore been enjoying free range, with a few exceptions. As before stated one of the main objects of the present law is to stop this. The law will be executed. And my opinion is that not only the State at large, but every section of the State will be benefitted. Your section will advance and develope with rapidity unprecendented. The stockmen will find room and security for his herd, without entering a scramble and contest for free range. The farmer will find the land adapted to his calling, always open for his entry, and free from squatter speculators or moonshine claims, and the man of the hoe, will soon be as numerous in reality as he will be or has been recently in fiction. In fact, my confidence in the near future is so strong that I feel at liberty to congratulate you on the prospects of the great north west. With kind regards.—

Very truly yours.—
R.M. Hall

References:

Amarillo *Sunday Globe News* Library, Amarillo, Texas

APPENDIX F

One of Temple Lea Houston's most noted speeches, yet of much less consequence than most, was unrehearsed, unprepared, and given when a meeting to nominate a candidate to serve Texas in the U.S. Senate began to lag. Temple Houston was quick to think and act with his speech given below.

SPEECH BY SEN. TEMPLE HOUSTON, NOMINATING SAM BELL MOXEY TO THE NATIONAL SENATE FOR THE THIRD TERM—WEDNESDAY, JANUARY 26th, 1887.

The president declared nominations in order, but the senators seemed loth to make them, each waiting for some one to break the ice. Several minutes elapsed when Senator Houston took the floor, and amid profuse silence nominated Hon. Sam Bell Moxey, as follows:

Mr. President and Senators—For the fifth time since the chains of federal despotism fell from her peerless form, Texas has come to claim her loftiest right, to name her choice for the national senate.

For the third time Texas has risen to judge the worth of the great man whose name I have the honor to place before you.

Texas demands a man whose intellect is commensurate with the vast trust imposed upon him, and whose name is a stranger to reproach.

To fulfill this high mission the man we send should unite every quality of worth and blend all the essentials of merit proven by trial. I will name such a man, great in mind, pure in heart, whose truth has been tried where spears are tried, and his works have known him. I mean Sam Bell Moxey! Christened by the fires of two wars, and true to every trust. He first, as a youth of 21, fought the battles of his country, and at Contreras, Cheruguesee and Chepultepec, beneath the eye of Winfield Scott, and beside Lee and Jackson, he was accounted spotless and brave, and was breveted on the battlefield. The Mexican war over, entering the legal profession he removed to Texas, and when the clarion warned her to man her warriors he cast aside all civic honors and proved his devotion to Texas in the front of battle—a test the brave alone may bear. Those of his regiment, his brigade, or his division who have seen him stand amid the falling forms of her slain sons, will not here deny his love of Texas or his title to her glories, nor say that, worthy to lead her soldiers in battle, he should not speak her voice in the councils of the nation. Whilst the black pall of reconstruction darkened o'er the land, and the shadow of deep grief filled the hearts of her sons, this man did not despair, but like a philosopher, held out the hopes of better days. The night passed, the storm was no more, and when the blue sky smiled through the rent veil of the tempest, Texas sent this man to the federal senate, and there his voice rang the reville of our redemption. In that day the prostrate south, and Texas especially were the marks of invidious legislation and ceaseless calumny. The great enemies of the south, were entrenched in the capital, and while Sam Bell Moxey, almost unaided and alone—for the south had few voices there then, rising to the full height of a senator of Texas, and speaking for her and toughern sisters, beat back the Xerxes hosts of flushed oppression and sectional hate. He was among the earliest to raise his protests against all forms of governmental extravagance.

When he entered the federal senate there was gathered there the brightest constellation of genius and talent within the republican party, and, although almost the only senator from a disenthralled state, in hopeless minority and beleagured by the myrmidons of hate, the man of whom I speak did not quail. He had fought for his country's rights on the crests of Chepultipec and with the same courage he battled for them in the arena of the national senate, and at the battle's close his sword knew no stain, and now a free south and a united nation answer his trusts. In twelve long years his record is flawless, and not a duty unperformed. Ne'er did knightliest crusader on the far sands of the Orient bare his blade, or place his good lance in rest with deeper favor or holier faith than has this man fought the battles of Texas.

And, in weighing him the third time in the balance, why should he be found wanting now, and never before? What reason is given? Is a single vote of his objectionable? No! Has he, of all the thousand trusts confided to him, neglected one? No! Is he in anywise unworthy? No! Reason should hang her head in shame at the suggestion proffered. Because he has had two terms! The very cause which enhances his fitness is quoted for his disparagement. Who ever heard of experience impairing, or of success disqualifying, a public servant? What encouragement will you give, then, to the youth for a faithful performance of duty? To heed this objection would be Athenian ingratitude and a sacrilege which I hope will never sully the fair name of Texas!

Were such a doctrine correct the victory of Fredericksburg would have removed Lee from Chancellorsville, whose crowning glories would not now beam around his brow; and Lord Nelson, because he won the Nile, would not have known Trafalger and died amid the deep thunders of his mightiest victory!

After twelve years of toil Gen. Moxey can say, as did the grandest apostle: "I have kept the faith!" No pledge violated; no promise broken, and his plighted troth as pure as when he give it. Call this man, the chief of her choice, and from her cities and villages and fields, from the east, where her pines, tall and dark, moan in the breath of the passing breeze; from the south, where snowflake never has fallen and the north wind chills not; from the rushing and radiant rivers of the west, from her long line of coast, where sounds forever the thunder of the sleepless deep; from her vast and silent plains, and from the virgin wilds of my own home, where the violet and wild rose bloom in the depth of her valleys; from yonder eternal mountains that saw the birth of light, whose brow has felt the kiss of every dawn and been bathed in the glories of all sunsets, Texas, with one glad acclaim will say: "Lo, ye have done well, for ye have chosen my worthiest!"

References

Sam Houston Museum, Huntsville, Files on Temple Lea Houston.

APPENDIX G

Temple Lea Houston was chosen to give the dedication speech during the daylong celebration of the opening of the new granite State Capitol Building on behalf of the citizens of Texas. Thousands of spectators thronged the grounds from the many steps of the building, from the windows of all floors overlooking the speakers platform, and as far as the eye could see in all directions. Approximately five thousand people watched the parade, listened to the speeches, and many of them thronged the House and Senate Chambers for the grand ball held in the evening.

The parade began at nine A.M. as the military marched up First Street followed by the mounted police under the command of Marshal Lucy. As many of the armed forces as could be mustered were in the parade.

At eleven o'clock Governor Ross rose and opened the ceremonies with a short address, followed by a prayer conducted by Dr. Wootan. Hon. A.W. Terrell was then introduced who welcomed the people to the ceremonies. Col. Abner Taylor then spoke to the crowd. Governor Ross then introduced the Hon. Temple Lea Houston, who received the new State Capitol Building on behalf of the people. His most impressive speech follows. Tall and handsome, his resonant voice carried over the throngs of people, hushed by the brilliance of his words and his magnificent delivery.

Seated on the speaker's platform with Houston were Governor Ross, Hon. O.M. Roberts, the Supreme Court Judges, General Mexia, General Stanley, and Hon. A.W. Terrell. In addition were distinguished officers of the Mexican army; Gen. Santos Benavides, representing the Governor of Mexico, Franco

Gonzales, Dr. Ornalee, Col. Richardo Villaneuva, Emilliano Corella, and Manuel Rivera.

SENATOR TEMPLE HOUSTON'S ACCEPTANCE SPEECH
May 18, 1888

The greatest of states commissions me to say that she accepts this building, and henceforth it shall be the habitation of her government. When the title to the noblest edifice upon this hemisphere thus passes from the builder to Texas, reason ordains a brief reference to the deeds and times that eventuate in this occasion. Texas has changed the site of her government oftener than any other state in this union, or any nation on this side of the globe. Prior to the transfer of this building the site of government of Texas has been changed eleven times; to-wit: San Felipe, Washington, Harrisburg, Galveston, Velasco, Columbia, Houston, Austin, Washington a second time, Houston a second time and Austin again, having been the successive seats of government of Texas. The state which to-day enters this building stands: First in Area, sixth in population, and seventh in taxable wealth among the sisterhood of states that comprise the American union. And when the tribes are numbered in 1890, she will stand third in population and fourth in wealth, and sit peerless e'en amid the proudest. She has a history all her own, wild, romantic, heroic. Minstrel's lay never told of deeds more daring than her sons have wrought, nor ever in castle hall hath harp of bard hymned praise of purer faith than that her legends bear. Child of storms, the nursling of revolutions, the twilight of her history made her soil the battlefield of freedom, her children the crusaders of liberty. Situated at a remote angle of the gulf, midway between the Aztec empire and the valley of the Mississippi, she for a while felt neither that spirit of Spanish conquest which laid in the dust at a blow the throne of Montezuma and the empire of the Incas, nor that gentle spirit of colonization which marked the footsteps of France and Britain upon this continent. But this repose was brief.

In 1522, shortly after the conquest of Mexico, the royal standard of Spain was unfurled upon Texas soil. DeNarvaez and his glittering calvary swept from the Rio Grande to Mobile. He paused not in his path. In vain might fairest valley smile or noblest landscape woo him but to stay; gold alone was deemed worth the Spaniard's while, and in this fierce quest he pillaged all the isles of the ocean and the two continents from California to the Patagonia. However, if the occupancy of the Pueblo of Isleta by Coronado in 1540 may be regarded as permanent, Texas was the first state of the American Union to be settled, and within her borders began that process of change that has transformed our country from a wilderness into an empire. But Spanish ascendancy remained inactive until excited by the jealousy of French encroachments. On January 1, 1685, Le Sieur Robert Cavalier De LaSalle, under commission from Louis XIV, landed upon Matagorda Bay. The object of the French was to establish colonies at the mouth of the Mississippi. The piercing mind of LaSalle saw that, from the Great Lakes, the trend of the watershed indicated the presence of a great valley in the center of this continent, drained by the mightiest of rivers, and he knew that this valley was the seat of empire. He knew that the measureless current on whose calm grandeur De Soto gazed was the same which Marquette saw, and De Soto, like Columbus died in pathetic ignorance of the extent of his discovery. How sad that so knightly a one should sink to sleep in the bosom of the great stream which he had perished to find, and know not whence came nor wither went the dark waters that over him rolled.

Winds and currents swept LaSalle westward and he saw Texas where the gulf in vexed magnificence breaks upon Matagorda peninsula. The Frenchman's colonial scheme was futile. Dissensions among his followers, want of support from the home government, hostile and intractable Indians, and, finally, Spanish intervention extinguished the last vestige of French settlement upon Texas shores. But when disaster had done its worst and the gallant Frenchman read upon the wall the handwriting of fate he did not quail.

Toward the upper Mississippi and the Great Lakes he therefore bent his steps. He crossed the Lavaca, the Colorado, the Bernard, Brazos, San Jacinto, Trinity and Neches. In the bottoms of the latter stream the cavalier was assassinated by his own followers. With him fell the last hope of French dominion in Texas. He, like the cavalier that he was, gave his life to his king and his God. Never crusader's cross blazed on a braver breast, and in knightliest tourney there rode no nobler spirit. In all the chivalry that shone around the throne of Louis, there flashed no fairer soul than he whose murdered form sleeps in the unknown wilds of the Neches forests, but his life and efforts were not without their results.

The French attempt at colonization roused the activity and jealousy of Spain. Grasping and ruthless as she was, Spain ever set religion's seal upon her conquests, and as soon as she had quenched the last spark of French settlement within the borders of Texas, she began the establishments of missions, resulting in the erection of about twenty institutions, dotting the valleys of the San Antonio, the Nueces and the Guadalupe; also, at Nacogdoches and on the San Saba. The noble order of the church, the Franciscan Fathers, reared there missions. Thou fathers, half priest, half knight, and all courage, lend a mingled air of piety and romance to the annals of Castillian conquest. In those missions showed both the censer and the sword, the mitre and the helm, for those pious fathers, in the spread of their Master's faith, dared the wilderness, but whosoever opposed their path felt the thrust of lance or the stroke of sword.

They came as conquerors. Nor did their name and deeds belie the martial name of their loveliest missions—San Juan de Espala. Within the portals of those missions might dwell saintliest abbot and holiest nun, but from their wall frowned Hispania's artillery, and at matins and vespers floated the melody of her bugles.

For more than one hundred years, the destruction of LaSalle colony until the stars and stripes rose above the Crescent City, upon the purchase of Louisiana, these missions were the seats of Spanish power and the center around which settlement clustered. Standing desolate yet beautiful, grand even in ruins, these old missions appeal to us with an eloquence beyond all words. They are the landmarks of a vanishing era, the boundary stones of a receding empire. They are the monuments of the mistaken zeal of a powerful and pious order.

The extensions of the limits of the United States to the Sabine River caused the concentration of Spanish military forces upon that stream. The interval between the purchase of Louisiana and the settlement of Texas by Stephen F. Austin is filled with turbulent events, but not sufficiently important in results to admit of extended mention here.

The same year which witnessed the final liberation of Mexico from her 300 years of Spanish rule, beheld the inception of the plan which resulted in the freedom of Texas, the colonization by Stephen F. Austin. The interval of fifteen years between the arrival of Austin and the independence of Texas is filled with events to which such brilliant and exhaustive reference has been made by that scholarly jurist, orator and statesman, who has preceded me, that any allusion from me would but mar the delightful memory that must linger of words that fell like pearls from lips so sage. But I will avert to one feature of that period. On March 1, 1836, the convention of the then province of Texas assembled at Washington on the Brazos. On the second day of its existence, that convention formulated a Declaration of Texas Independence, which, in literary merit, challenges comparison with the finest productions of our language. That same body of men in fourteen days prepared the constitution of the Republic of Texas, which remained for nine years, without a suggested amendment, the organic law of Texas.

It should not be forgotten that this constitution was framed amid an overwhelming invasion, that participation in the proceedings of that convention was threatened death, and that those who drafted that constitution laid down their pens to grasp the sword; that it was indeed born amid the clash of arms and rocked in the cradle of war. The beneficence and perfection of its provisions, the rapidity with which it was prepared and the reverence with which it was obeyed, make the constitution of 1836 one of the evidences that Anglo-Saxon race is capable of self-government. The men who devised that constitution were the apostles from Runnymede, they were the disciples of Jefferson, they were the evangelists of liberty, for, wherever that race breathes, on land or sea, oppression ceases instantly.

The principles which they proclaimed at Washington on the 2nd of March, 1836, they, fifty days later, at San Jacinto, sealed with their blood.

It was the old conflict between the Latin and the Teuton. It had been fought between the armies of Arminius and Varus. It had been battled when the Armada was dispersed, and at Trafalgar and Waterloo, and fate had decreed that the Anglo-Saxon should triumph, for wheresoever on the face of the earth this knight-errant of liberty plants his foot victory has greeted him and Christianity has been his companion. (Here Houston's speech was interrupted with great applause.) When the last hour pealed, its sounds rang from a spot where the Republic of Texas died, where the state of Texas was born. On yonder hill, where the clock chimes each fleeting hour, once stood an historic building—which now only lives in the memory of a venerated few. In a log building on that hill the pioneer legislators framed the constitution of 1845, under which Texas was admitted into the union. When the seat of government was located here in 1839, this point was beyond the extreme outposts of the frontier. But the sublimity of the scenery, the majestic beauty of the spot, marked it as the place ordained by fate as the capital of Texas, and such shall it ever remain. (Again applause interrupted Houston.)

The people of Texas are indebted to United States Senator Charles B. Farwell and his brother John V. Farwell, of the firm of John V. Farwell & Co., of Chicago, and Colonel Abner Taylor, not only for the best statehouse in the United States, but more especially for bringing our public lands into worldwide notice, by agreeing to build the house for the 3,000,000 acres set aside for that purpose. It will be recollected that these lands were offered for sale at fifty cents an acre, without attracting purchasers, while the building has cost nearly three times fifty cents an acre, and is really worth more than five times that amount, if we are to measure its value by the cash cost of similar buildings in other states.

The state and the Farwell syndicate are to be congratulated on such a result was demonstrating, beyond the power of successful criticism, the wisdom of a contract which made it possible. The state, because she has realized for these lands much more than she could have done under her land laws for their sale and got them under tax, and at the same time secured the use of this noble building for all time, which probably would never have been built in any other way. The syndicate, because they have obtained 3,000,000 acres of the best land in Texas, and will in due time cover them with prosperous farmers and increase the wealth of the state by hundreds of millions of dollars, instead of leaving them for the free use of foreign cattle companies whose earnings would not have remained in the state.

Every true and honest Texan must rejoice that the Farwells have found a way to turn our previously useless land into such a state monument as we are this day dedicating, and that they must from self-interest—if no other motive—cover these lands with farmers, as soon as railroads have opened them up. From every point of view, therefore, I say emphatically, as a true friend of Texas, whatever may have been thought by critics, that we have but done better than any of us thought, and the Farwells are justly entitled to our thanks, and this celebration by this vast concourse of our citizens is the best expression of our feelings toward the men who have made it possible. This magnificent building will speak for their skill thousands of years after we have ceased to speak. And when the state, in its citizens, shall realize a value in these lands, improved and settled up, of $10 to $75 per acre, no one will say that the Farwells were not entitled to every dollar they will make as a just reward for benefits received by the state.

In 1852, by the sale of her title to New Mexico, Texas occupied the capitol which was destroyed by fire in 1881. Let us not pass lightly by that old structure. Its halls knew so much of the grief and glory of Texas, so much of her splendor and her sorrow, and so often saw her destinies alternately flit between triumph and ruin. Within the walls of that old capitol, whose buried foundations rest yonder, the government of Texas was administered for twenty-eight years. Beneath its roof were assembled thirteen legislatures and four constitutional conventions. There were framed the constitutions of 1861, of 1866, of 1859, and of 1876, the organic law under which we now live, and containing the provision of the erection of the capitol in exchange for 3,000,000 acres of the public domain. Within those walls, since wasted by fire, passed much over which the historian of Texas must ponder. It was there that a fair fruits of annexation withered beneath the simoon breath of war. Here, too, in frantic haste was consumated the act which shattered the golden links welded by sixteen years of union, and hurled Texas into the vortex of secession. And after Southern Valor had wrecked itself against the might of the union, that same old capitol, on whose ruins many of this multitude stand, saw reconstruction plait its crown of thorns around the weary brow of Texas and press the sponge of bitterness to her lips. Yet that same old building saw the departed Sceptre return to Judah when the Fourteenth Legislature calmly grasped the reins of power and submitted the constitution under which we live. In the adoption of that constitution you, the people, decreed the erection of the building which you to-day accept and dedicate to your use. It decrees the eternal union of Texas. Hereafter let no man seek to put asunder that which the fathers united. Let the fiends who wait upon the lost hiss their hate and shriek their curses in the ear of him who would plot the dismemberment of Texas. To-day is an era in our history: The survivors of the early struggles who view this building realize that all which they did was not in vain. Texas stands peerless amid the mighty, and her brow is crowned with bewildering magnificence! This building fires the heart and excites reflections in the minds of all. It stands alone the haughtiest type of modern civilization.

In other lands the hand of man hath reared walls as stately as these and pierced the sky in prouder heights. The architecture of a civilization is its most enduring feature, and by this structure shall Texas transmit herself to posterity, for here science has done her utmost. The quarry has given its granite and marble and the mines have yielded their brass and iron, and an empire has been passed as an equivalent for this house. All that enlightment and art could do has been done. Were I to repress the

121

reflections that occur to me now, I would be untrue to my convictions and to this occasion. It would seem that here glitters a structure that shall stand as a sentinel of eternity, to gaze upon passing ages, and, surviving, shall mourn as each separate star expires. Were we to feel thus, precedent would justify us. Those who builded the Pyramids thought the Egyptian empire eternal; those who reared the Colesseum boasted that it was a pledge that Rome was everlasting. More solemn lessons are taught at our own doors. Great races have swept o'er the bosom of the deep, and left traces almost as faint. Who reared the Pyramids of Uxmal, the palaces of Palenque, the mausoleums of Mitla? The splendors of towered Tulum. What is the date, the origin, the fate, of those mysterious civilizations that have vanished forever in the forests of Mexico and Central America, and that flee from the searcher like those illusive lights that flash and fade above the silent tomb? They were our predecessors. Shall oblivion fling her darkening pall over us? Ah! we are but one of that vast procession of races which it was decreed should pass across this hemisphere. We have no right to say that our own is the first or the last of those civilizations whose impress it was ordained this continent should feel.

More than once the world has lost and resumed civilization. If our civilization possesses the elements of perpetuity it differs from any of its predecessors. If the lessons of the past have not been taught in vain, they tell us that the future holds in hands an hour when the curious antiquarian shall wander through the roofless chambers amid the shattered arches and fallen columns of all their imperial magnificence, and ask when were these walls reared—was this edifice, place or prison tomb or temple? Does it seem impossible? Balbas's marble columns are as proud as these, yet who chiseled them? Who carved the hieroglyphics that plead for interpretation from the sculptured walls of Planque? The past hath a fearful lesson of the instability of earthly greatness. Men dwelt upon the earth thousands of years ere they ascertained its shape. They proudly claim an existence of 6,000 years, yet their annals do not include half of it. They cannot explain their diversity in language, or the secret of their existence. The destruction of public virtue caused the decline of other

122

civilizations, but does our civilization carry with it the means of its perpetuation? Under certain conditions it may. It possesses characteristics that mark none of its predecessors and particularly can this be said of the state of Texas.

The civilization of Texas, of which this proud capitol is one of the voices that shall speak to after ages, is beneficent. The form of our government is the creation of an expressed wish of the people whom it affects. The officers are elected and are the servants, not rulers, of the people. We have no obligatory form of worship, our rights of free speech have no limitation; before our laws all men are equal; our government is a subject of criticism, not of hideous dread. Our armies and fleets are for the protection, not oppression, of the people. Our institutions enjoin an education of the masses, and assume that the government is not the heritage of one man, but the property of the people. Texas says to whomsoever casts his home within her benignant realms, she tenders his offspring an education without money and without price. This education is given to whatever child that abides within her border.

No matter what race may shame its origin, or what reproach clouds it birth, Texas pledges 35,000,000 fair acres and twelve and one-half percent of her taxable values, amounting to millions, that every child that asks it at her generous hands shall receive a free education. The first government of the earth to enact the homestead exemption in favor of the family, she stands pre-eminent in her beneficence to the helpless. Within sight of this structure are the grand charities which Texas bestows upon the blind, the deaf and dumb and the insane; she also has remembered the orphan, and her statutes provide for the indigent. All these would indicate a perpetuity of public virtue. This noble edifice is a fit seat for such a government. It and the features of our civilization are all we can leave our posterity, and, even should they prove unworthy of our bequest, we can at least pass from life's stage with the proud reflection that we leave behind us a purer civilization and a nobler edifice than has been bequeathed to us by preceding ages.

References

The State of Texas, Library of Congress, Published by The Texas Legislative Council in Cooperation with The Texas Highway Department, Austin, Texas, 1967.

APPENDIX H

Temple Lea Houston received a letter from the staff correspondent, F.S. Banle, of the *Star*, a newspaper printed and published in Guthrie, Oklahoma, requesting a copy of the following speech to be given before the Bar Association meeting to be released only after the speech had been delivered. That is probably the reason this particular speech was preserved outside the annals of the Bar Association minutes. This speech concerns a trip Houston made probably in late 1897 or early in 1898.

AMERICAN CIVILIZATION

by Temple Houston

The subject which I have chosen is one upon which more patient yet, fruitless research has been bestowed than any in the catalogue of scientific questions. Despite all of the long centuries of investigation spent upon it the subject still remains wrapped in painful and impentrable mystery. A mystery that darkens and deepens as time sweeps on and one conjecture after another proves false and theory after theory is overthrown. After all, this should not seem strange. Let us pause and remember that at the time of the discovery of America the idea of the rotundity of the earth was ridiculed—and beyond the mediterranean basin and the European coast west of Denmark—not a 20th part of the Earth's surface—the rest of the world was unknown to civilization.

The Portuguese had just discovered the passage around the Cape of Good Hope thus destroying the Oriental caravan trade, and wrecking the maritime and commercial importance of Genoa and Venice. The martial zeal and religious fervor of the

PARTIAL reproduction of speech in Houston's handwriting.
—*Courtesy of Mrs. Mary Henderson, reproduced from aged original by Ben Pilcher, Abilene, Texas.*

crusades still thrilled Europe and the intellectual awakening kindled thereby yet convulsed all classes of men. "Stony Gallilleo" had read the glittering message written in the skies and the magnetic needle made the mariner feel safe in the wildest of seas. It is not generally known but true never-the-less that the object of Columbus in his first voyage was to procure by conquest the means of procreating a New Crusade for the recovery of the Holy Sepulchre at Jerusalem.

All learning was practically confined to the church and here is the beginning of our difficulties.

In that age all military expeditions were accompanied by a retinue of priests who with all the vast learning which they undoubtedly possessed were wild fanatics and bigoted beyond all imagination. These, upon the discovery were dumbfounded at finding two mighty continents, whose surrounding seas were gemmed with countless isles—All containing a dense and in some instances a refined and civilized population, and who it seems had not been included in the plan of salvation, originating in Judea 2000 years ago. These pious fathers were the antiquarians and historians of the early expeditions and all that we know of prehistoric civilization as it appears at the discovery is refracted through the uncertain medium of their superstitution and prejudice. To them all variant form Christianity was abdominable and of Satan and everything in conflict with their notions of scriptural truth was false and altogether evil. Their purpose was to destroy the idols and temples of the Indians, to obliterate their worships and to extinguish the last vestiges of a religion and priesthood in which was the entire history and traditions of the aboriginal people. Hence all we know of primitive America is dim and shadowy. As an instance of how this fanatical zeal carried the ancient fathers it is related that Zamarroaga, the bishop of Mexico, shortly after the conquest in 1523, collected from all over the Aztec Empire every manuscript, both of hieroglyphic and picture writing that was possible to procure by imperial power and have them all gathered into one massive pile in the plaza of the city and burned. The pyramid of ancient literature thus formed was of gigantic proportion and its destruction was a calamity to Science and mankind, second only to the loss of the Alesandrian library through the barbarous zeal of the Caliph Omar. Doubtless these manuscripts so ruthlessly annihilated contained an elucidation of much that must now forever remain unknown, mayhap they explained the presence of man upon this hemisphere, and revealed the mystery of Atlantis and the last told to Plato by the Priests of Heliopolis. So far has this destructive zeal been carried that today we do not know the boundaries of history of either the Aztec or Peruvian Empire although at the conquest both had a recorded history written laws and a civilization more elevated and refined than that of their conquerors, and so far did this proceed that no one can read either the Toltec or Aztec hieroglyphics in the Peruvian Quippus, through such were perfectly intelligible to the natives at the time of the conquest.

The contemporaries of Cortez doubtless could have read the glyps that beseech interpretation from the chisled altars of Capan, from the sculptured walls of Palenque—Long after the overthrow of the Inca Empire there survived Peruvians who could render into language the annotated and colored cards in which the laws and history of that frailest and most evanescent of civilizations were preserved, and when misguided fervor of religious zealots has thus effaced so many memories of the civilized nations of America—how little can we hope would be preserved to us of the cruder and more Barbarous tribes that succumbed to the arts and arms of the invader?

When Hernando DeSoto, the discoverer of the Mississippi River, between the years of 1541 and 1542 traversed this continent from Florida to the probable vicinity of Natchez, Mississippi, he found it peopled by a bold warlike and semi-civilized people but the relations of his companions refer only to battle, Marches, Massacres and pillage and do not enlighten us to much which the antiquarian pines to know. Now as we know all the great Mississippi today especially on the eastern side is thickly dotted with prehistoric mounds, built for the various purposes of defense, worship, and burial, and from their excavation has come the little that we know of our racial predecessors on this continent. Now strange to say neither the French nor Spanish explorers of the Mississippi tell us whether or not the Indians whom they found in possession of the continent were then using and occupying these mounds or whether they were the Indians or whether they were of a mysterious race whose origin and fate are lost in far away depths of the remote past. A certain unity of design and similiarity in location and construction of the Mississippi Valley mounds would indicate that they were the work of one people who in distant ages held sway in the valley of the great river. This theory is strengthened by chronological pecularities common in skulls found in such mounds to say nothing of a resemblance in pottery and implements and singular sameness in the mode of interring the dead. The past that the discovery of the Mississippi Valley was peopled by hundreds of different tribes having nothing in common, speaking different languages and entirely of diverse races would preclude the supposition that they as their ancestors built mounds, and in all likelihood had they then been used as fortifications, temples or tombs, the chronicles of the discoverers would doubtless so inform us. The great valley abounds in imposing aboriginal structures such as the great Serpent Mound at Marietta, Ohio, and the Cahokia Mound opposite St. Louis, Missouri, and all the early explorers say regarding them is simply discriptive. They offer no conjecture as to the antiquity or purpose, such silence is inexplicable unless we assume that they considered the subject profane or were inundated with so many mysteries that they omitted reference to these. But it is fair to assume that these structures reared by a mighty religion, numbering its devotees by the millions would not have been forsaken without a long and bloody struggle, such as really occurred further south, and that when the conquerors came, DeSoto and his compeers, these temples had long been worshipless, the flames in the altars dead for ages, the very gods abandoned and forgotten and these strange mounds then as deep mysteries to the Indians as now to us. Modern research elucidates some of these perplexities. Fortunately for Science southern Mexico and Central America at least these portions that most abound in prehistoric ruins have been thoroughly explored by profound and gifted archaeologists, notably among them John L. Stephens accom-

panied by the artist Cathermond, Baron DeSire Charny, E.G.
Squier, Duboise and Waldcott, and the ruins of vast cities, of
whose very existence the world was ignorant, have been laid bare
and exposed to the gaze of an astonished universe.

Certainly several of these cities were as large as modern
London or Paris, in estimating their size we should bear in mind
that only the temples, the public building, the palaces of the
kings and nobles survive and that the lesser buildings con-
stituting the habitations of the great majority of the people have
perished utterly long ago. In fixing the antiquity of these ruins
we are absolutely without reliable date, but a few faint gleams
of light flash through the darkness as follows:

The loveliest group of all American ruins, Palenque, is
situated in the Mexican state of Tabasco in the delta of the great
Usmamacinta River, the mightiest stream on the hemisphere
between the Mississippi and the Orinoca. Now its ruins attest
that in the days of its occupancy its population might have approached the millions, in 1524 on his famous expedition to
Honduras, Hernan Cortez passed within three leagues, less than
twelve miles, of the present ruins and there established the town
of Los neu Cruces, still existant. This authentic history, now had
the great city of Palenque been then inhabited Cortez would
have undoubtedly heard of it and after the goodly custom of
these gay old days turned aside and plundered it. Hence we
must infer that at the time of the discovery of America Palenque
was desolate, and as completely buried from the knowledge of
men as if it had been like Pompeii, covered by the lava of
Vesuvius. It was only in 1722 that its ruins were accidently encountered in the depths of the tropical jungle. Palenque is rich
in hieroglyphic inscriptions and strange to say at Uxmal and
Yucatan at Capan in Honduras distant five hundred miles the
same character of architecture and hieroglyphics appear. Now at
the conquest and even yet the intervening space is peopled by
different tribes of Indians presenting even no difference in
language, physiognomy and traditions, and all pathetically ignorant as to origin of these stupendous ruins, showing that
neither they nor their progenetors knew aught of them, and
here occurs again the strange silence of the annals of the con-

querors as to any connection between the aboriginal races and these massive structures at the time of the conquest. Among the best preserved groups of ruins in America is that of Uxmal near Merida in Yucatan. It is contended with some degree of plausibility that it was still occupied at the time of the conquest of Yucatan in 1542 by Don Francisco Muteje and the grounds of the contention are as follows:

An old deed or "Fitalo" from the crown of Spain to Don J.M. Peon in whose family the title to the grant still rests. I have seen a copy of the deed and it recites among other things that the grantee undertake to suppress the idolatrous worship which it was known that the Indians openly and notoriously performed in the buildings and trocallis, whose ruins we yet deplore, the deed in refering to "Vinery of Siegen" sets out that the grantee went into and through the buildings and opened and shut the doors and drew water from the wells (Aquada y Norias) indicating that the wells then ran water and that the now desolate and ruined buildings then had doors that could open and close, but the lawyer would naturally suspect that Don Peon imposed on his royal master anti idolatrous practices in order to secure the grant and that the opening and shutting of the doors and drawing water was simply a passage in the deed copied from some well established precedent the occasion and significance of which the loyal mind readily grasps and even if, at so late a date, a few despairing priests of a waning religion still clung around their gods and altars, it would only show the date of abandonment and not of the erection of these mournfully beautiful ruins, No, such cities as Palenque and Copan and Taloom and Uxmal would not have yielded with a struggle as fierce as that which marked the fall of Mexico, and the fact that there was no such struggle shows us that these great cities had long since ceased to be even memories at the time of the Conquest. This is one of the saddest spectacles in all of history, of Mesopotamia, Assyria, and Egypt we know much despite the lapse of four thousand years. Out here is a vast empire, with all that empire implies, the fire of eloquence, the rapture of poetry, the lovliness of woman, the glorious courage of man, all swept beneath oblivious waves, leaving an eternities waste, not a vestige. There shines not a name of her heroes, not a word of her language, not a deed of her sons, her perdition is often as if the great Toltec Empire had sunk with Atlantis beneath billows of the Mediterranean Ocean.

Our Indians, the Cliff Dwellers, in the United States never attained anything approaching the civilization reached further South in the Tropics, the little we know of them has been revealed by their buried mounds, regarding whose antiquity are conjecture is folly and concerning which as before said history and tradition are silent.

Their weapons were of a primitive kind and tipped with either bone, copper, flint or obsidian, the presence of copper and obsidian in mounds far distant from where either of these articles are produced coupled with the extensive prehistoric mines in the copper regions of Lake Superior show conclusively that our predecessors on this continent had a wide spread and far reaching commercial relations with each other, beside this there is only one place in the United States where this re-like clay, so common among Indians is produced, in Minnesota, I believe. Pipes of this material are found in Indian graves all over America. As stated before their diversity in language, religion physiognomy and tradition added to their racial antipathies preclude the possibility that they or any of them could have been even the remote progeny of the mound builders, who were probably driven from the Mississippi valley and revived their culture in the tropics, only to perish in any manner that will never be known.

Gazing on these stupendous ruins of lost and forgotten empires let us remember that they in their pride doubtless thought themselves as great as children of the earth could become. Where are they now? So may it ever be with us, for our works are of the land earthly and the failure may hold in hand an awful hour when the curious antiquarian shall wander through the deserted streets of our mightiest cities and standing on the ruins of our own structures, wonderingly as in a now unknown tongue, who were these people and whence did they come and whence did they go.

References

Sam Houston Museum, Huntsville, Texas, Files on Temple Lea Houston.

APPENDIX I

It was lovingly dubbed "The Castle On The Hill" by loyal friends and students because it was patterned after the castles in other countries. It was the dream of the first president of Northwestern, Dr. James E. Ament. As modern standards go it was not particularly efficient as a school building. It was built largely of wood and its interior was destroyed by fire in 1935.

Temple Houston was asked in 1898 to dedicate a building for the Northwestern Territorial Normal School (now Northwestern State College) Alva, Oklahoma, for the new school of higher learning for which he had helped to get money appropriated and donated. The first classes were held in 1896 with two hundred and eleven students enrolled. In 1899, when it was completed, classes began in the old "Castle."

To Houston it was an edifice of progress, a monument to former educators as well as an institute of higher learning.

Special mention in preserving this speech and seeing that a copy was placed in the museum should go to Mrs. Beulah Owen Starr and Joe Edwards. There is a prologue to the speech that lightly but sincerely covers the "Castle," the university, and the development of the college and the city of Alva, Oklahoma. To keep the record intact, this too is included in this chapter.

ADDRESS BY TEMPLE LEA HOUSTON

The following address was made by Temple Houston, son of Sam Houston, President of the Republic of Texas and the first Governor—having helped to free Texas from Mexico, and having been very active in the annexation of Texas to the United States.

134

The occasion for such an address was the dedication (laying of the cornerstone) of the first academic building for the Northwestern Territorial Normal School. This event occurred at Alva, Oklahoma Territory, on July 1, 1898. This building was lovingly called the "Castle on the Hill" by all loyal friends of the institution—but more particularly by the students who entered its halls and especially by each of Northwestern's graduates who came to revere it as their very own. This name was a "natural" because the architectural design was that of an old European castle—the dream of Northwestern's first president, Dr. James E. Ament. This building remained the material image of all the aspirations and ambitions of students and friends—until its destruction by fire in 1935. Judged by modern standards it was about forty percent efficient as a school building—built largely of wood in its interior, it was also an easy victim of the fire which destroyed it.

Soul-hungry sons and daughters of the pioneers who had settled this "Cherokee Strip" in 1893 came to Northwestern seeking not only to build their own characters but also to acquire the training to enable them to go forth and teach a still younger generation of children who were to be found on the farms and in the villages of this area.

Alva was only a prairie village nestling here on the banks of the Salt Fork of the Cimarron River. However, on the history-making day of this dedication, more than six thousand men, women, and children had traveled by wagon, cart, buggy or perhaps on horseback to stand in grateful and almost reverent awe, while the cornerstone was being laid, and this speech was given. These thousands stood patiently and gladly on the rich cushion of browned "buffalo grass," as a gentle summer breeze brought these words from the speaker's platform.

Not only the beauty and the dignity of this "Castle on the Hill" but also the promise of days yet to be were emphasized and glorified by this speech and in the hearts of the hearers.

Morton H. McKean
(Class of 1912)
Alva, Oklahoma
February 11, 1966

"CASTLE ON THE HILL" which Houston dedicated. —*Courtesy of Northwestern University, Alva, Oklahoma. Reproduced by Ben Pilcher, Abilene, Texas.*

SPEECH MADE BY TEMPLE LEA HOUSTON

We have assembled here to consecrate a structure to the noblest, the most beneficient of all purposes—the education of mankind. The edifice whose cornerstone we today lay is more than a mere educational institution. It is one designed for the special instruction of those who have dedicated their lives to the science of education itself.

No superstitious rites, such as the ancients observed, mark these ceremonies. All that takes place here is upon a soil trodden only by the feet of freeman and is accompanied by the invocation of the ministers of a religion that preached the universal brotherhood of mankind; the immortality of the soul, purity of life, and penalties and rewards hereafter, for deeds done in the flesh. And besides, this very stone is placed by the hand and under the auspices of that ancient and illustrious order that more than all other earthly insitutions has preserved throughout all the world the precepts of the Holy Scripture and righteousness among men. This event occurs at a most auspicious moment in our national history and at a time that will be very memorable in our annals, for even now the nation is engaged in a most momentous war with a power that once ruled the very soil on which these walls stand, and while we are gathered here in the sunshine of peace our brethern are engaged in freedom's struggle on the far shores of the southern seas.

It might be expected that in response to the invitation with which I have been distinguished that I would bestow much of the space accorded me to the question of education, especially considering the character of the edifice. But after what has been said and beautifully said by the learned and distinguished educators who grace this occasion and after the profound and entertaining references to that subject by the distinguished officials, whose presence honors us, it would seem supererogation on my part to make more than a passing allusion to that exalted science, and I shall discuss those questions which are almost born of this very hour, and which must affect deeply the destinies of those who teach and shall be taught when this magnificient building shall tower in its completed glory.

The ground on which these stones rest, within historic times, has been owned by England, France, Spain, France again, and the United States and under extinguishable title by the Cherokee Indians and again in full Sovereignty of the soil by the United States. On September 16th, 1893, it became in all that such implies an integral part of Oklahoma Territory. Prior to the date last mentioned it had been the hunting ground of the Indians, the grazing land of these true sons of Ishmael—our western cow man. Even as Old Eden was guarded by fiery sworded Cherabein waving all away who came near, the federal soldiery with presented steel kept back the pressure of the advancing settlers who sought this garden of promise. The land was in a state of nature, solitude reigned, the bald eagle built his ayrio high among your dizzy crags and watched his nestlings fledge with no dread of man's approach and the timid deer sipped the crystal waters in the cool depths of your dells with never a fear of the hunter's stealthy tread. Here fearful storms spent their wrath; they burst above the lonely canyons, their restless lightenings flashed and faded unseen of earthly eye and the deep roll of their thunder died unheard on mortal ear. The want of presidential power waved and as if by instant enchantment a wilderness became an Empire. On every side at the same instant the envisioning lines broke over the border, and who were these settlers? and hence came their lineage, and institutions. Look at them carefully. Every state in the Union is represented and the child of the cavalier stands beside the descendant of the puritan. They speak the tongue of Milton, and they bring with them the laws of Alfred, the philosophy of Frances Bacon and the religion of Jesus Christ. They are empire builders. As far back as the mystic scroll of history reaches their ancestors were freemen, and they are the real evangelists of liberty, for wherever they abide they rear temples to their God and by their side spring up houses for the education of their children. These men bring with them, even as their bear their hearts in their breasts, their inalienable rights, a written constitution, which must certain the right of trial by jury, the writ of habeas corpas, the free press, the inviolable sanctity of person and property against aught save due process of law. These are the children of the men who established this very government, who in their sublime march pierced the Alleghenys, crossed the Mississippi, penetrated the Rockies and only for a moment passed on the golden shores of the Pacific. Every nation on earth has felt the empress of their might and genius, and this occasion, arising as it does on a spot that less than five years ago was a wilderness, these thronging thousands, with the patriotic pride which they seem to feel in all that transpires here, shows that our heritage of enlightened liberty and of all that secures it is still unimpaired.

Despite all the incalculable benefits certain to accrue to the entire territory from the completion of this structure a wail of anguish has rent the air over the legislative action in providing for it and even over the action of the educational board in undertaking to carry out legislative intent.

The last legislature of this territory passed the law by virtue of which this building is commenced and made due appropriation therefore. This was done only in the face of fierce opposition. Whatever uncertainty there may have been in the legislative mind, there was none in the executive, and when presented to him, Governor W.C. Renfrow, to his honor be it said, signed the bill and on the 12th day of March it became a part of the law of the land and binding upon the inhabitation thereof, the willing and the unwilling alike.

His Excellency, C.M. Barnes, signed his approval to the contract carrying the law into effect, he having cast the deciding vote in the legislature that gave the West a school.

It is a pleasure and pride to realize that his Excellency has shown himself above a sectionalism and that he is the Governor, not of a part, but of the entire territory, and is the friend and a patron of higher and universal education.

As was intimated a moment ago since this stone was laid in a memorable year that will be signalized as the one in which, with the rod of retribution Spain was scourged from this hemisphere, and also as the one in which our nation casting away the traditions of a century entered upon an irresistable career of territorial expansion, and here upon a spot devoted to education, education the only sure safeguard of liberty, we may with all due appropriateness to this occasion pause and solemnly ask "Is this departure frought with danger to republican institutions?" Let history answer. "Green withes and cords that were new and strong" would not bind matchless Sampson. Neither should traditions and theories of more than a century ago hamper this nation in attaining a destiny the most glorious of history. A policy of isolation, wise for thirteen struggling was undeveloped and whose government was still an experiment would never control the greatest people whose armies are invincible and whose iron navies now make the nations of the earth tremble.

Speaking of sanctity of traditions it should never be forgotten that the three greatest steps in history of this nation were at the time they were taken regarded as violative of the constitution and of the spirit of our institutions. I refer to the purchase of the Louisiana, the annexation of Texas and the abolition of slavery. One was regarded as reckless extension of our domain beyond the borders of the original area of the thirteen colonies the second as the incorporation of the independent nation into our system, the third as a violation of the fundamental condition of our union, and yet time has vindicated the wisdom of these measures, any one of which would have been ruinous if undertaken at the time of the foundation of the government, when the policy of isolation of which we now hear so much was inaugurated, what was wisdom then might be folly now.

When I was a child, I spoke as a child, understood as a child, and thought as a child, but when I became a man I put away childish things. (St. Paul 1 Cor., Chap. 13, Verse 11.)

Our government at the incredibly low price of $1.50 supplies a map of the nation, thereon clearly defined the boundary and date of each of our territorial acquisitions, as follows: Louisiana 1803, Florida 1819, Texas 1845, Mexican cession 1848, Gadsen Purchase 1852, Alaska 1868. This map should be in every school of the territory. Doubtless each of their territorial acquisitions was opposed by the same elements that now seek to avert the Nation's march in the roadway of glory, opposed with the same motives and happily with the same results that will retard the present attempted repression of national development.

To prove that territorial expansion foreshadows national ruin, we are cited to the examples of Rome and Spain. No similitude exists. Those two powers indeed vastly extended their boundaries over subjugated nations and therein found the ruin. But what was the condition of the people over whom they spread their sway. Over whatsoever people the Roman Eagle glittered their liberty perished instantly, and all territorial acquisitions of the imperial city were designated as provinces and the rulers who robbed them and the soldiers who kept fast their fetters, all came from Rome. Roman laws might be extended over an unhappy realm, but they were for the Roman alone and the poor provinces groaned beneath a bitterness of bondage of which this age can never conceive. The provinces had nothing in common with the central power, and when corruption and luxury sapped her vitality, as they will of any people, and the blue-eyed man of the north came down her rule was shattered at a blow, for in her structure the element of concession was wanting, and with the decay of her military power the bonds of her domain shrunk back to the shadows of the seven hills, where the wrecks of her might still moulder. Similar in the great drama of Spanish history when the almost dynamic valor of her sons had subdued nine-tenths of this hemisphere and the golden standard of that proud power floated o'er a vaster sway than was ever held by any nation in earth's annals, what was her course? All the frightful atrocities of pagan conquest the unspeakable horrors of the Goth, vandal, Turk, or Tarter invasions melt into nothingness compared with nameless cruelties with which for three centuries Spain tortured the nations of this and the southern continent, when an inscrutable decree of fate had confided to her crown. The very life blood was wrung from the veins of her victims to swell the might and magnificence of the ecclesistical and temporal power of which Madrid was the center. Her colonies were in reality provinces, her haughty sons only visited them to plunder and slaughter their inhabitants and return to Spain glittering in treasure that almost meant a life of every doubloon. Like those of her preceptress, Rome, her colonies had nothing in common with the mother country, and when Napoleon laid the weight of sword upon Spain her colonies fell from her, even as a tree casteth her untimely fruit, leaving her in this the hour of her extremity desolate indeed. Interrogate history once more. What has been the course of Great Britain toward her colonies? It is true that our ancestors taught John Bull how colonies ought to be treated and the lesson was not lost. Whatever British power has been planted British laws and British liberty accompanied it and British colonies constitute an inseparable part of her empire, and in all her tremendous wars her colonies have never wavered in their loyalty and nothing but that loyalty enabled her to sustain her titanic struggle with the great Napoleon, even when Europe was prostrate at his feet, for to her the sea was open, in that hour Britania through her colonies ruled the waves, else who would not now exist as a nation. The contrast between Latin and English methods of treating colonies explains the significance in those chapters in history. Consult our maps, and what has been our treatment of our territorial acquisitions, such as to link them to us by hooks of steel, for they are truly taught to regard the union with all its glories as their own. But we have no alternative. We must accept what destiny offers us. Under the conditions of modern naval warfare we must have our stations distributed properly throughout all the seas. The great destiny that confronts us came unsought but it is here and we must meet it worthily. If our mission is of the character claimed for it, we should be inferior in no respect to any earthly power. To stand still is to retrograde.

Recent developments have immeasureably enhanced the importance of sea powers, in fact, except as between contigous nations it is paramount. We must provide for all visable contingencies. The recent enunciation of international law regarding coal as being in a measure contraband of war leaves us in my opinion no option as to whether or not we shall retain our conquests, soon to be completed in Cuba, Puerto Rico, and the Phillipines. Their retention gives us an assured naval and military preponderance in the waters which they command. We should not disregard the divine command, under which I believe, this nation is impelled. Having conquered these islands a certain degree of responsibility for their future attaches to us inevitably. We can not, if we would, evade it. Would not these islands be happier, purer, more peaceful and religious if beneath our gentle sway, than if left to their own fierce dissentions, or turned over to the pitiless powers already assembled, hungry to oppress and devour them. Upon the answer to this question depends our duty to God, to them and to ourselves, and in closing this portion of these remarks I wish to quote in reference to the dangers to this government of territorial extension, the words of one whose lofty patriotism no one can question. I refer to the words of General U.S. Grant in his inaugural of March 2, 1873.

"In the first year of the past administration the proposition came up for the admission of Santo Domingo as a Territory of the Union. It was not a question of my seeking but was a proposition from the people of Santo Domingo, and which I entertained. I believe now as I did then, that it was for the best interest of the country, for the people of Santo Domingo and all concerned, that the proposition should be received favorable. It was, however, rejected, constitutionally, and therefore the subject was never again brought up by me. In future while I hold my present office, the subject of acquisition of territory must have the support of the people before I will recommend any proposition looking to such acquisition. I say, here, however, that I do not share in the apprehension held by many as to the danger of government becoming weakened and destroyed by their extension of territory. Commerce, education and rapid transit of thought by steam have changed all this. Rather I believe that our Great Maker is prospering the world in his good time to become one nation, speaking one language, and when armies and navies will be no longer required."

On the occasion of his second inaugural President Jefferson used these words in reference to the purchase of Louisiana.

"I have said, fellow citizens, that the income reserved enabled us to extend our limits; but that extension may possibly pay for itself before we are called on; and, in the mean time, may keep down the accruing interest. In all events, it will replace the advances we have made. I know that the acquisition of Louisiana has been disapproved by some, from a candid apprehension that our enlargement of territory would endanger its union, but who can limit the extent to which the federation principle may operate effectively? The larger our association the less it will be shaken by local passion; and in any view is it not better that the opposite bank of the Mississippi should be settled by our brethern and children, than by strangers of another family? With which would we be most likely to live in harmony and friendly intercourse.''

So, when Jefferson and Grant, the two greatest exponents of their respective parties agree on the safety of a doctrine it should be followed if there is anything in precedents.

I mentioned a moment ago a map supplied by the government which shows the dates and boundaries of all our territorial acquisitions, there is one addition and the greatest, which is not shown on any map. I refer to the late southern confederacy. No greater or more perfect conquest was ever effected when this nation received back to its bosom the seceded states and all that dwelt within them. It performed an act which through the long flight of ages will be spoken of as a memorial of perfect goodness and as wisdom unexamplified among men. When within the surrendered lines of Lee's heroic army Grant told him, ''Let your men keep their horses, they will need them to raise their crops.'' He spoke as a prophet and unconsciously ushered in the reconciliation that now exists. No such spirit was ever shown before between warlike man. These words were spoken on the very battlefield, bloodily won, and would have been impossible in all the ages that preceded them. They could only have been spoken between Americans. And if the great soldier who spoke those words can now see his son serving by the side of the confederates, Fitzhugh Lee and Joe Wheeler, all in Union uniform and the stars of a general glittering on the shoulder of each, he feels that his pathetic and simple message, ''Let us have peace'' was not uttered in vain and that the nation whose unity he so grandly preserved is one indeed, for all time. I know that no doctrine contrary to such sentiment will ever be taught within these walls.

Let no blow now meditated be struck at this institution. Whoever purposes such should pause. Her educational institutions and their marvelous success are the glory and the pride of this territory. They should be increased, not reduced. With a logic that must convince they show to the world what we are and what we offer to those who will abide with us for the purpose of rearing their offspring and enjoying the delights of a refined and intellectual society.

Let no selfish or misguided hand mutilate even the humblest of our school houses. The people of this territory love all their schools and view with no friendly eye an assault on any of them. You might as well try to take from this territory the groves that crown her hills or the streams that gem her vales as to injure one of them—even the lowliest.

Our young territory, not yet adorned with the coronet of statehood, can say in her institutions as did Cornelia, the mother of the Gracchi "Silver and gold precious stones wear I not," But pointing to her noble children, "these are my jewels.

Blessed with all heavens bounties, facing a future rich with immeasurable possibilities, if we are true to ourselves, what a noble destiny awaits this fair young territory. Her history, though short is replete with progress, courage, goodness and wisdom. Even now her broad fields are mantled in the golden glories of her mighty harvest, her rivers radiantly are rolling down toward the silvery sapphire sea, her valleys all are glad and her countless hills rejoice, her sons are so brave, her daughters so fair, who shall tell the splendors of her future? You might as well seek to loose the bands of Orion or solve the sweet influence of the Pleaidos.

Reference

Northwestern State College, Alva, Oklahoma, Museum Bulletin No. 1966.1 (Second Duplication, March 25, 1971).

APPENDIX J

Whenever he appeared in the courtroom or in a celebration dedicating a monument or building, crowds gathered to hear his words, his imcomparable wit, his sincerity, and his abounding intellect spoken by a man who was considered most handsome by the ladies of the day and in a voice that rose to a dramatic crescendo and fell to a low confidential and caressing tone in line with the words he spoke. It is no wonder he was asked to give a speech to a large group in September, 1897. He chose a current and controversial subject of the day, astronomy. With his knowledge and research on the subject he hoped to clarify many points as well as educate against superstition, and to entertain.

Space age development of the science of astronomy has disproved some of the older beliefs and has proven others as the fact, that the moon is unhabited. This contains valuable information and as compared to today's knowledge, is in many cases, documented with space travel.

As you read, picture a tall man, very handsome, well groomed, even a little eccentric, in white Mexican type bell-bottom trousers, a frock tail coat and black tie, his brown hair curling slightly on his shoulders. Picture, if you will, his flashing grey eyes and how they held the audience of approximately one thousand people, all spellbound, anticipating with great pleasure, his next words.

He began his speech by reciting a couple of short poems in tune with the words to follow.

146

LECTURE ON ASTRONOMY

by

SENATOR TEMPLE LEA HOUSTON

Woodward, Woodward County, Oklahoma, September, 1897

Ye Stars, which are the Poetry of Heaven
If in your bright leaves we would read the fate
Of men and empires 'tis to be forgiven
That our aspirations to be great
Our destinies o'erleap their mortal state
And claim an kindred with you—for years
A beauty and a mystery and create
In us such love and reverence from afar
That fortune, fame, power, life, hath
    named themselves a star.

                  —Childe Harold.

*****Blue the sky
Bespangled with those isles of light,
So wildly, spiritually bright.
Who ever gazed upon them shining,
And turned to earth without repining,
Nor wish't for wings to flee away
And Mix with their eternal ray.

                  —Seige of Corinth.

LECTURE ON ASTRONOMY   By Senator Houston

    Of all sciences astronomy is the oldest. In the dim and morning twilight of earth's history where the gray and gold of the dawn mingle the gaze of mortals has swept the deep and purple vault of night, vainly seeking to read its glittering mysteries. In the pure transparent air and cloudless skies of

147

Mesopotamia the Chaldean Shepherds for long ages watched the sparkling orbs that flash in the boundless immensity of space and bathed their souls in the light of the stars until their spirits seemed touched with celestial radiance; and the stars bore to them a mystic meaning that they alone must read. And the Shepherd Priests, the earliest astronomers, told that the Deity wrote his purposes and his messages to earth in the signs of the stars; and astrology became a science, not yet extinct. The Bible, composed as it is by a Semetic race and near where astronomy began and passed its infancy, is full of the evidence of this superstition which it justly condemns. In fortelling the desolation of Babylon, the cradle of this sublimest science, Isaiah says, "Thou are wearied in the multitude of thy councils. Let now the astrologers, the star gazers, the monthly prognosticators, stand up and save thee from these things that shall come upon thee." In Genesis God said to Abraham, "Look now toward heaven and tell the stars if thou be able to number them," and in Judges in the song of triumph over the defeat and death of Sicera, Deborah and Barak say "They fought from heaven, the stars in their courses fought against Sicera." The inspired writers also believed in the eternity of the stars as witness the Prophet Daniel when he exclaims, "And they that be wise shall shine as the brightness of the firmament and they that turn many to righteousness as the stars forever and ever." The darkest evidence of divine anger is shown in the stars as Joel tells us "The sun and the moon shall be darkened and the stars withdraw their shining," and in his threatening of Egypt, Ezekiel writes "I will cover the heavens and make the stars thereof dark, I will cover the sun with a cloud and the moon shall not give her light." In cursing the day of his birth Job cries out, "Let the stars of the twilight thereof be dark, let it look for light but have none neither let it see the dawning of the day." And in fortelling the last day the Saviour says "And there shall be signs in the sun and in the moon and in the stars, and upon the earth distress of nations, with perplexity." And St. Paul says, "And when neither sun nor stars in many days appeared, and no small tempest lay on us all hope that we should be saved, was then taken away." The stars were also regarded as symbolic

148

of purity, by both the profane and sacred writers. To give us a most exhalted idea of the unapproachable holiness of God the poet says, "Yea, the stars are not pure in his sight," and in the most awful sublemity of the last chapter of Revelation Jesus says, "I am the root and offspring of David and the bright and morning star." And then too the herald of Christ's first coming was a star. For in the book of Numbers we read, "There shall come a star out of Jacob and a sceptre shall rise out of Israel," And the wise men of the East seeking the infant Savior ask, "Where is he that is born king of the Jews for we have seen his star in the east are come to worship him?" And in the same chapter, "Lo, the star which they saw in the east went before them till it came and stood over where the young child was. When they saw the star they rejoiced with exceeding great joy."

Early Eastern Nations, even the Jews themselves, were strongly inclined toward a worship of the heavenly bodies for in the ten commandments occur the words. "Thou shalt not make unto thee any graven image, or any likeness of anything that is in Heaven above." And in the book of Deuteronomy God warns his people thus, "Take ye therefore good heed unto yourselves * * * * * lest thou lift up thine eyes unto heaven, and when thou see'st the sun, the moon and the stars; even all the host of heaven be driven to them and serve them which the Lord God has divided unto all nations under the whole heaven." And Stephen, the first martyr, reproached those that slew him reminding them that, "Then God turned and gave them up to worship the hosts of heaven." And further saying, "Yea, ye took up the tabernacle of Moloch, and the stars of your god Remphan, figures which ye made to worship them."

Doubtless at some time in their development every race of people have been sun worshiper.

The knowledge which the ancients acquired of astronomy is surpassingly wonderful; they had no optical instruments to aid their observations, no magnetic needle, neither calculus or trignometry to prove or perfect any calculation; their sole basis of computation were angles and shadows; the periodical changes of the celestial bodies. Yet from these, with the naked eye, and their knowledge of geometry, they ascertained the procession of the equinoxes, the rotundity of the earth, and that it, with some of the nearer planets, revolved around the sun. The Egyptians, Hindoos, Greeks and Chinese all made out that the year had three hundred, sixty five and one-half days, and the record preserved by the three latter races, of more than five hundred eclipses, has been verified by modern research. That with the most primitive instruments and few of them; and scarcely any scientific aid, this degree of advancement should have been attained is a glorious commentary on the strength of mortal mind.

The first authentic fulfilled prediction of an eclipse, however, was made by a Greek, Thaler of Mileteus, six hundred and forty years before Christ, and according to Herodatus, this eclipse put an end to the war between the Medes and Lydians. The knowledge of astronomy possessed by the ancient Peruvians and Mexicans was surprising, as each of these people had constructed a calendar of considerable accuracy but many of their notions of heavenly bodies were pitiful superstitious, and both were sun worshipers, and such, some of their descendants yet remain.

It were wearisome for me to relate the slow advance of astronomy from its beginning to its present proud eminence, but sufficient to say that after the fall of ancient civilization with the Roman Empire, astromony suffered in common with all science, and with the destruction of the Alexandrian Library, the greatest calamity in all history; and the long night of the dark ages that hung over Europe, the knowledge of the stars, acquired by so many long ages of watching and toil, almost faded from the earth.

But with the revival of learning, a new impulse was imparted to this science; the ancient knowledge that had survived the wreck which Europe had suffered, was collected; super added to this was the lore preserved through countless centuries, by the Chinese and the East Indians. And at this juncture, rising out of the desert, the Arabian mind shed its sudden, strange splendor on our starry science, bringing to its aid algebra, the mother of calculus, conic sections and analytical geometry; and by the close of the crusades, nearly all of the lost progress had been regained, and then came the invention of the telescope, and discovery of the magnetic needle, and with these, modern astronomy became possible, and the glories of the heavens were unveiled. If a mortal proud of intellectual power, wishes to feel how finite, after all, are the mightiest minds, such should attempt to conceive of the infinitude of space, for like the eternity of duration, space is boundless, having neither a beginning nor an end.

Constantly are telescopes being enlarged, and their magnifying power proportionately increased. But as far as the most powerful lens can pierce in the remotest depths of space, millions of shining worlds never dreamed of before, crowd on the searcher's enraptured gaze. Even many of these filmy clouds of light that we long thought were but nebulae—cosmic dust illuminated by some mystic light—the great tubes now tell us are suns, and systems of suns, countless billions of miles from our little world. And if we had started for them at the earth's creation on a ray of light, at the rate of 200,000 miles a second, we could not now see that we had approached any nearer them. And as space in the nature of things can have no limits, it is fair to presume that it all occupied by worlds, throughout, as in our own stupendous universe. When we seek to grasp this thought, how frail and helpless does mortal mentality seem? Despite the swift and gigantic strides made in astronomy by modern appliances, we can claim an extensive acquaintance with none but those heavenly bodies, that in common with our earth, revolve around the sun. You will pardon a brief reference to them here. As you well know the mean distance from the sun to the earth is 93,000,000 miles, and the earth moving in an elliptical orbit performs her revolution about that luminary, within three hundred and sixty five and a fraction days. Throughout the solar system the sun is the source of light, heat and energy, all of which is undergoing a steady, ceaseless source of exhaustion. Our little earth is nearly eight thousand miles in diameter. The sun is 852,000 (nearly a million) miles in diameter. About one hundred and six and one-half times greater than that of the earth. So if you were to take a baseball and a bird shot you would have nearly a correct idea of the relative sizes of the sun and the earth.

For many ages the sun was thought to be an immense globe of boiling, seething fire in the highest state of combustion, and disseminating its light and heat universally, in all directions throughout space. This idea is long since abandoned. It is not certain that the entire surface of the sun is hot; but it is surrounded by a gaseous vapor and its interior is in a molten and eruptive state. Occasionally flames 70,000 miles in length are instantly projected into space, from deep disturbances beneath the crust of the sun. And at periods of partial regularity immense fissures and ragged cavities called, "sun spots" form on the white and quivering surface of the sun. And some mysterious and as yet, unexplained relation exists between the cyclonic disturbances on the earth and the presence of the spots on the disc of the sun. These sun spots, so astronomers and meterorologists tell us, likewise cause the gorgeous and exquisitely beautiful display of auroral lights around the poles of the earth. For you must know that both the sun and earth, the moon, and all heavenly bodies, are powerful magnets. These solar spots are frequently sixty to seventy thousand miles in diameter; ten times larger than the Pacific Ocean. So if our world were to fly the track and be drawn to the sun, striking one of these spots, as smaller bodies frequently do, it would drop into the interior of the sun, without touching the edges of such a tremendous aperture. The sun transmits no heat to the earth. It simply excites magnetic heat already here, left here ever since the earth was formed from chaos, out of the cosmic dust floating in space. Baloons carrying register thermometers, ascending in the tropics on a hot day to great altitudes, bring back a registry of eighty degrees below zero. If simple contact with the sun's rays were enough, the loftiest mountains beneath the equator would not be white with ever-lasting winter, and inaccessable because of intense, deadly cold. No, the magnetic properties of the sun's rays striking the surface of the earth at a right angle in an atmosphere of sufficient density will excite heat, but rarify the air, and diminish the angle of the rays, and the heat immediately lessens. Were the axis of the earth to shift ninety degrees, everything in the Amazon valley would freeze almost instantly, and the tropical verdure bloom at the poles. The same

152

thing virtually is thought of light. The radiance of the sun does not fill all solar space, but if you could soar above the illuminated air of the earth, say five hundred miles, where atmospheric particles cease, you would be in the blackness of midnight, for there is no question as to the fact of intesterstellar darkness and the sun world only glows with a dim, dull glare, if at all. Go down on the brightest of days, into the depths of a coalmine and look up and the stars are all shining as brilliantly as at night. No, light is no more than heat transmitted, it too, is magnetically excited.

There are certain electric currents that radiate from the sun to every member of the solar system, even to the comets, astroids, and possibly some of the largest meters. Through the channels of these enormous currents the reciprocal forces and influences of light, heat and electricity, flow back and forth perpetually between the scepted sun and his tributary orbs. But outside of these currents is the blackness of great darkness and possibly the elastic, tenous, indefinable ether, that pervades all space; for we can not conceive of a place where there is absolutely nothing, except in a dude's skull. Nature carries her abhorrence of a vacuum throughout all space. If, as was once claimed, the sun shot out his light and heat uniformly throughout space, he could not sustain such a draft on his energies ten minutes. And this stream of light and heat poured steady upon the earth, undisturbed, to say nothing of ultimately extinguishing the sun, would turn the earth to ashes in a day. Where would the sun get his fuel—unless the sinners of Oklahoma go there? and besides that it would be a waste of power; something that nature forbids. No, outside of the shining pathways of the planets and comets, space is a realm of sunless gloom. Our sun only warms and lights those whom the Maker confided to his care, and the surrounding immensity is still wrapped in primeval darkness. But the sun has plenty to keep him busy. He has to stay in his office all day and he can't run around with the boys any at night—and I sympathize with him. Besides the mean distance of the planets from the sun is as follows: Mercury 35,392,000 miles, Venus 66,143,000 miles, the earth 91,430,000 miles, Mars 139,311,000 miles, Jupiter 475,692,000 miles, Saturn

872,137,000 miles, Uranus 1,755,869,000 miles, Neptune 2,754,998,000 miles. Jupiter is the largest of the planets, its diameter being 85,000 miles. A year on Jupiter is equal in length to twelve years on the earth; that is Jupiter revolves about the sun in 4,332 days. A year on Saturn is equal to twenty-nine years on the earth. A year on Uranus is equal to ninety years on the earth; and a year on Neputne is one hundred and sixty five times as long as a year on the earth. There are near one hundred comets, two hundred asteroids and a greater stream of meteors, to say nothing of the planetary satellites, and invisible and yet undiscovered celestial bodies that with sublime precision perform the regular journeys around in elliptical orbits about the sun. Not a crash, not a collision, not an instant's delay, but with a harmony possible with God alone. So that the Greeks believed that for Him on High, they made a melody which was called the 'music of the spheres' and the oldest of all remembered poets breaks out in rapture hyming, when the morning stars sang together, and all the suns of God shouted for joy. My audience is too familiar with the size, distance, peculiarities and properties of the planets for me to weary you with details regarding them, but with your indulgence, I will refer briefly to certain interesting data concerning them.

I don't mean by that the Rings of Saturn, and his and also Jupiter's squadron of moons, and the canals of Mars. But Mars has nearly as many hours in a day as the earth, and plainly has a habitable atmosphere, with rolling seas, oceans, tides, and storms, and seems little if any, dissimiliar from our earth in the conditions that surround him. He also has ice-caps at the extremities of his axis. The atmospheric conditions and light properties there are ascertained by a process known as the Spectrum. Wherein his light beams are retracted magnified and subjected to an analysis. The method employed is to extensive to enlarge upon here, but all the quantities and properties of his air, as that of any other planet, thus studied, are faithfully revealed. This process applied to other planets, Venus excepted, fail to show the existence of habitable conditions upon them. In fact it almost negatives such a possibility, unless the beings that might dwell on such bodies, are totally different from all forms

154

of animal life here. Jupiter, like Mars, was known to the ancients. He is larger than all the other planets and the satellites combines; in fact all of them put together do not equal two-fifths of the mass of Jupiter. In giant size and luminosity, Jupiter resembles the sun, and may be an ancient and expiring sun, that has wandered into a sphere of solar attraction. So great, however, is the magnetism of this mighty planet, that early in the century, when it was fartherest from the sun, and on the remotest outer edges of the solar system, he drew from another universe one of its comets that came too near him, and then swept past him, wheeled around the sun, and disappeared forever in the trackless deeps of outer space. Neptune and Uranus were not known to the ancients, but are recent discoveries as I told you awhile ago, but in 1846 astronomical instruments were far fewer and less perfect than those we now possess, but on account of the perturbations visable in the movements of Uranus, astronomers surmised the proximity of a powerful and disturbing element, and for three years could not determine its nature or locality. Finally the observatory at Berlin, then having the largest lens, was advised on a certain evening to search a designated region of the heavens, and true to the letter, Neptune passed beneath the sceptre of science. The last found was the most distant of all the planets.

Between Mars and Jupiter, distant from the sun between two hundred and four hundred million miles, are about two hundred little planets called asteroids; all of them united would not equal one-fourth of the mass of the earth. But long before the discovery of a single asteroid, the prescient eve of science has in the regular progression of interplanatary distance, from the sun to Uranus, recognized a great gap between Mars and Jupiter, and supposed that the space was filled by a lifeless opaque planet, and when at last one after another of the asteroids were discovered, the theory became accepted that a proud planet, once took its haughty flight within that space, and was shattered by some frightful convulsion, that must have made the very sun tremble upon his burning throne. And these are but shattered fragments of a destroyed world. And it may have been a world fairer than our own; for often the loveliest are the lost. It would be unfair to leave the solar system without a reference to our nearest heavenly body, the moon, and too she is a lady, though she has less to say than most of her sex. In a lecture on geography delivered three years ago I made some reference to the moon, but do not be frightened, I will not repeat them. I won't repeat them, it would look too much like you did not believe what lawyers said. The recent Jerkes telescope with a lens nearly six feet in diameter brings the moon, for observation purposes within fifty miles of us. And it is conclusively shown that she is a dead planet. Her atmosphere has vanished, her oceans and seas are dry. The fires that once melted her surface with fervent heat have expired and departed, and the "Silvery Queen of Night" is but the cold corpse of a star. Yet once rivers made her valleys glad and all her hills rejoiced, broad oceans thundered their surges against her shores, earthquake shook and rent her surface, and mighty volcanoes hurled their pillars of fire far into the azure depths of the air, that mayhap mortals breathed; maybe kings and empires lived their little day upon her breast, and were, but are not. Was she wicked, and the Maker judged her in His wrath, as He did the guilty cities in the valley of the Dead Sea? Or is she but gone the way reserved for all worlds in their time? What became of that fierce energy that once swayed her, what became of her air and her water? Her mighty central fires that tore the chasms in her continents, and cast up from her depths, her terrific volcanoes? That energy was dissipated somewhere in space leaving her dead, bleak and desolate as the earth, sun and planets, in the fullness of time may become. All that remains to her, is her fearful magnetism, in which she is most truly feminine. She still rules our tides from artic to antartic and her attraction for terrestial objects exceeds that of the sun twenty times and her influence on our weather is predominant. And as we all know the word lunatic is derived from the malign influence, which at certain phases, she exerts upon the worst forms of dementia. Now I have confused insanity with the solar system, I had best change the last branch of this subject.

In addition to the solar system are the fixed stars. Stars whose distance is so great that their movements are almost impreceptible, and who have no known relation to our system. These stars seem never to move. If the old Chaldeans, after a lapse of five thousand years, could come back and look upon the heavens again from watch towers in Babylon, they could not perceive the least change in the relative position of these stars. As they appeared to Abraham, even to Noah and Adam, so do they now serenely shine down upon us, after the lapse of so many thousand years. Why is this? The nearest fixed star is two hundred billion miles from us, if not more, and it takes light traveling at 180,000 miles a second, nearly five years to traverse that distance. If a railroad train flashes near by you, it seems to travel very rapidly, but look at the same train twenty miles away, and it hardly seems to move. Carry that principle into the millions and it is easy to understand why the fixed stars appear stationary. Their distances are only approximations, there is nothing determinate in the results achieved by the very largest telescope. These measurements are made by a very simple system. It is only a gigantic method of triangulation—as you all doubtless know. If we wished to find the distance from here to the water tank, it is not necessary to step it. Take an observation here, and measure off fifty yards, and take another, call the fifty yards the base line. We know the angles the object describes with the extremities of the base line; the length of the base line, and the rest is simply a matter of trigonometrical commutation. Astronomers know the distance in a straight line from the Cape of Good Hope to London and by taking contemporaneous observations of a planet at these two places they have their base line and two angles. This is called stellar parellax. It was successful on the planets and their satellites and the most distant comets. But when applied to the fixed stars no angle was perceptable. They then sought to take observations at the same time from the earths surface nearly opposite each other, thus using the 8,000 miles diameter of the earth as a base line. And still the stars would not reply. Then observations were made six months apart from the extremeties of the major axis of the earth's orbit giving them a base line of 180,000,000 miles. This could only be an approximation, and the star selected was 60Cygni, supposed of all the fixed stars to be nearest the earth. A barely perceptible parallax rewarded this effort. And the estimated distance of a limited number of the fixed stars has been imperfectly estimate. But their study in other respects, has been more fruitful of results. The spectroscope and large telescope turned upon them bring tidings that dazzle the soul. We find pairs of stars revolving around each other, called binary stars, and many of the fixed stars that shine with a pale lustre, on examination present hues as variable as the colors of the rainbow. Some are blue, others purple, green, yellow, pink, orange, brilliant red and violet, and many glow with a golden yellowish splendor; and yet others shed the white brightness so notable in Sirius in the nose of the Canis Major, or the Great Dog. Fearful catastrophes are often beheld in the deeper heavens among the fixed stars. There many a noble star has been seen suddenly to blaze out in unutterable brightness for years, and then slowly to relapse in darkness, the death of a radiant world. In 1572 Tycho Brache, the great Danish astronomer, says, "A fixed star in the constellation of Cassiopea instantly shot rays of splendor undimmed by the glories of noon, brighter than all the planets, and refused to hide his head in the presence of the sun and was visible to the naked eye in the meridian of perfect day." It held its place in the heavens sixteen months and slowly waned, darkened and disappeared and has never been seen since. It's distance was immeasurably great and no parallax could be taken. It was a 'wandering hell in eternal space,' or in the language of the Bible, "Wandering stars to whom is reserved the blackness of darkness forever." A similar phenomenon in 1604 appeared in the constellation of Ophinous, and after a few months, in like manner, vanished forever. As was intimated earlier in this article, all visible fixed stars are conceded to be suns. Presumably the centers of systems as vast or vaster than our own. So we do not behold a billionth of the bodies that occupy the space seemingly filled by the stars that we really see.

On account of the immense distance traversed by light, in traveling from the fixed stars to us, there are stars whose light seems yet to shine upon us, that were darkened and extinguished long ages ago; and there is now on its way to us light from other worlds, newly created that has not yet reached us, for every year fresh glories take their place in the "star isled seas of heaven." Despite their immense distances, the velocity of the fixed stars in many instances have been ascertained with appreciable accuracy. One of them constellation Groombridgy, star number 23, moves at the apalling speed of two hundred and forty-eight miles a second. Our earth only moves about eleven hundred miles a minute, but this star travels at the rate of 892,800 miles a minute. But with even our earth, to say nothing of this rapid star, such tremendous velocities can only be explained on the supposition that the heavenly move through a nonresisting medium, and also evidence the operation of giant attraction. The Rev. Jasper, a negro minister of Richmond, Virginia, was right, "The sun do move," but his velocity is not known, but he is rapidly traveling and carrying with him his satellite train of meteors, comets, and planets. The point toward which he directs his course is a star known as Lambda Herculis, a bright star in the constellation Hercules, in the northern heavens, and toward there, systems other than ours, are bending their way. Hence doubtless there is situated some grand central sun around which myriads of systems perpetually wheel, and seated thus in the lonely sublimity of space perhaps this mightier sun with his vassal systems in his train, with other outlying suns similar to himself, revolves around a still grander and more remote center, and it may be that this progression advances until we reach the source and center of all created and existent nature where seated upon a throne of ineffable splendor, with the signs of his power furled in awful glory about him dwells an invisible, infinite First Cause. Astronomers opine that the Milky Way is but an extension infinitely of the universe, and that really we and all other heavenly bodies are in the Milky Way and that it continues endlessly throughout space. Just north of where the Zodiac crosses the Milky Way is the Greak Black Vault and unlit immensity, and if there is end of the universe it is visible through that great starless vault that leads to outer darkness or is the opening into another universe of which we cannot even conjecture. Of all these things the anxious soul that thirsts for knowledge, must remain in pathetic ignorance until the spirit has answered the last summons and opened the portals of eternity, but all things teach that these innumerable worlds sparkling far and near throughout fathomless space were made for our good and to teach the existence, beneficience and power of Him, faint flashes of whose brightness shine radiantly around the angel form of the one who all ablaze with celestial glory awakened the weary shepherds of Galilee and amid the soft low strains of heavenly music said, "On earth peace, toward men good will."

Woodward, Woodward County, Oklahoma
September, 1897   Senator Temple Houston

References

Amarillo Sunday News Globe, Library, Files on Temple Lea Houston.

APPENDIX K

Temple Lea Houston delivered the Centennial Address at Nashville, Tennessee, May 1, 1897. He said in preparing his speech it would be his best effort.

TENNESSEE CENTENIAL ADDRESS

No state in the Union—No—nor has the same space of earth elsewhere borne itself more gloriously than Tennessee. In arms, in jurisprudence—in literature—in all that constitute excellence, she has no superior.

Not to name, the way in which here unaided she won their way over the savage from the mountains to the shores of the great river and tendered to this nation a free and redeemed commonwealth—she won other titles to immortality.

Thrice—in the deepest lines has the life of this nation been held in the hands of Tennessee.

At Kings Mountain she pulled back the tide of disaster, and from the union of that—the revolution became a success and the current of human history changed.

At Chalmette the fatal arm of her riflemen repulsed the last invasion of the soil of this nation, but more than that we owe her a greater debt.

When the inquisition of a corrupt and false system of finance became apparent, the greatest of all Americans, Andrew Jackson, in her strength and courage, laid his right hand upon Bible and read his history in the nations eyes.

The first European to enter Tennessee, was the Adelantado Hernando DeSoto in the year 1540-42. The chronicles of his meanderings describe the then inhabitants of this region as of matchless bravery, devoted to their native soil and preferring

161

death to subjugation. Their bright characteristics still adorn with an undiminishing lustre your People.

Spain—beyond the contingent grant to DeSoto, of the realms he might conquor, fraguily termed "Florida," never asserted claim to any portion of Tennessee. The past ambition of DeSoto and the Chimenical claims of his soveriegn at midnight in the Great River, discovery is the sale title to immortally won by DeSoto—thus within forty-nine years after the discovery of America was Tennessee traversed by the Spaniards. Doubtless the first definite assertion of claims to the land embraced within the limits of Tennessee by a European Sovereign was on March 24, 1663, when Charles granted to Edmond Earl of Clorlaba, and others all the region between the thirty-first and thirty-sixth parallel of north latitude from the Atlantic to the then unknown Southern Sea, which now so well deserves and beautifully bears the name Pacific. This swept from the Alleghenys, across the Father of Waters, plains, across the Rocky Mountains. Even to the coasts of that mysterious Southern Sea, whose blue and gentle expanse had then hardly borne a European vessel, but that was the beginning of Anglo Saxon dominion in Tennessee.

More than one hundred and thirty years after the death of DeSoto, no Caucasion foot step pressed the soil of Tennessee but the Grant of the Dissolate Charles II was bearing seed.

In 1665 pioneers had pierced the great Blue Ridge and looked with rapture upon the lovely panorama spread before them. There pioneers and who of them erected the first habitation within your border we have no exact information nor do we even know the precise route taken by them.

In 1573 Marquette from the vicinity of the Great Lakes reached the Mississippi and descended it to the Gulf and passing your Western boundary, like infrequent visitors, was charmed with the beauty of the scene. Nine years later the great LaSalle, with forethought of mind founded a Fort and a trading post near where the historical city of Memphis now stands, the first structure erected by civilized man within the bounds of Tennessee. Strange coincidence that this same settlement can undertake * * * * * (part of speech unable to translate from original).

The treaty of 1763 renounced to England * * * * * that portion of the nation. But already glowing reports brought back by traders and trappers added to the restless impulse. So worked in the Anglo Saxon pioneer had started the streams of immigration from the Atlantic through the gorges of the great Appalachian Chain.

But Military possession of the country was never taken from the British nor was any form of government attempted for the region. It was still practically unsettled. Primeval Nature was undisturbed. Solitude reigned. Then as now your forests became green beneath the breath of Spring and withered in the winters blasts, but gladdened never the heart of civilized man. Here fearful storms spent their wrath but the trembling savage, thin restless lightenings flashed and faded unseen of earthly eye and the deep roll of thunder died away unheard of earthly ear.

So England's sceptre never swayed there vallies, her standard never floated from their mountains, their realms never knew despotisms pollution. God dedicated your land to liberty and whatever may betide others only bear yourselves in the future, as in the past and you will always be free.

So three great nations claimed Tennessee, but none ever ruled her. She was not one of the thirteen colonies, yet strange to say as mightily as any one of them did the free and fearless arm of her sons untie the shackles of the British oppression from the Atlantic shore. Certainly her people were the very Evangilists of Liberty.

The passed and great Appalachian Chain in quest of New realms, and were happy there, and yet at freedoms call they turned back and at Kings Mountain the iron courage and the deadly aim of Tennessee riflemen broke the crest of British invasion.

It is a historic error to say that the battle of Saratoga eventuating in the capture of Burgoyone is one of the sixteen * * * * * of the world. Kings Mountain established the Revolution and determined its result. The Chain of British invasion from Georgia to the Mississippi broken at * * * * * and with * * * * * British Supremacy at this time begun to wane.

Despite her brilliant part in the Revolution and the dangers

163

that menaced her borders the admission of Tennessee into the Union was long and unnecessarily delayed. The opposition to the Admission was the first definite expression of the portentious conflict between the slave and free states of this nation which culminated at Sumpter.

Virtually having fought her way into the Union, she bore herself worthily.

References

Amarillo Globe Library, Files on Temple Lea Houston.
Sam Houston Museum, Huntsville, Texas, Files on Temple Lea Houston.

AUTHOR'S NOTE: It is obvious from both copies received that this speech was taken from some old handwritten manuscript or a newspaper clipping that had been weathered so badly that portions were very difficult to transcribe. With apologies to the State of Tennessee for the incomplete copy, I felt that it should be noted that his devotion to that state was as strong as his devotion to the Nation.

APPENDIX L

Father Kamp and Temple Lea Houston became very close friends and often visited together even before Houston embraced the Catholic faith. This devotion is shown in the eulogy below given at the funeral of Temple Houston.

FUNERAL ORATION DELIVERED BY REV. FATHER KAMP

A TRIBUTE TO TEMPLE HOUSTON

Looking around me, I see people of every station and class in life gathered around the bier of our departed friend. The feelings of sympathy and interest manifested by you are a tribute greater than which it is possible for me to give to him. Your presence here speaks for him. Actions speak louder than words. The very fact of your being here shows that our departed friend was held in esteem and reverence by you.

We deplore today the departure of a man who, humanly speaking, should or ought to have lived longer—a man of a mighty and powerful intellect; a man who was a promoter of this place, whose activity for the good of his fellow men was great and whose labor for the welfare of the community was unceasing. But this active and laborious life has been brought to a close.

The once busy hands are folded upon the silent breast. The tired brain no longer toils and plans. That mighty intellect, which in days gone by scrutinized the profoundest problems and most difficult cases and solved them, works no more. The loving heart, ever willing to do good to its fellow men, has ceased to beat, but the memory of many, nay, of all who knew him, he still lives.

I have loved wisdom and pursued it, and in it my heart has rejoiced. To know things, to know the "ins" and "outs," the "pros" and "cons" of every case brought before him was the aim of his life. To use the knowledge, acquired after hours of hard study, for the good of his fellow men, was his greatest pleasure. We all admire wisdom, we all admire intellect, we all admire brains, but when a man uses that wisdom and intellect for the welfare of the community at large, and of each of its members in particular, then we honor, revere, esteem, love such a man. Our departed friend was such a man. He was genius "sui generis." Would to God that his mantle could be thrown on the shoulders of some of our citizens to make of Woodward what he would have made of it if he had lived longer.

During his lifetime he allowed himself but few leisure hours, and no doubt it was to him a source of great pain that he was called from life to desist from his labors. But in various ways limits are put to an active life.

First: The insufficiency of bodily strength. We can go only so far as our strength will allow us; beyond it we can and must not go.

Second: Then there are various sicknesses. Many things can be accomplished by the strength, power, cleverness and intellect of man when he is well, but when sickness seizes his frame in its merciless grasp he can do nothing, a limit is put to his active life.

Third: When the years of youth and manhood have passed and old age creeps on, the time of labor is over; another limit to an active life.

Fourth: Finally death, the ultimate limit to an active life. This is the night of which Christ speaks, when no man can work. The night cometh, etc. Blessed is he who has labored in love for his fellow men and who, in faith and hope, has prepared for his salvation in time. This, again, our friend has done. When sickness threw him upon the bed of suffering, when the time of helping his neighbor had passed, he began to think of himself. Before, he was all for all and all to all. But now he gave a few moments to himself. Realizing that this life is not all, but only a preparation for a life to come; realizing the words of the poet, that . . .

166

"Life is real, life is earnest,
And the grave is not its goal;
Dust thou are, to dust returnest,
Was not spoken of the soul."

Realizing all this he began to prepare for the last hour, for that ordeal through which every living man must go; which, again, he did with the same earnestness and energy, as he had worked for others. And having accomplished that work, he gave, with perfect resignation and love, his soul to his God, from whom it came.

Living and dying, he has built himself a monument—not of brick and mortar, not of stone or frame, but a more lasting monument of love in the hearts of many. If we could gather around his coffin all those who have experienced his goodness, there would not be room enough for them. What would they do? What would they say? Profuse gratitude and thanks. Many a tear of thanks and sympathy would roll down their cheeks. And what would be the effusions of those whom he has delivered from the very chains of prison or from an ignominious death? I leave that to your imagination.

The love of God is the first and greatest commandment, but the love of our neighbor is alike to it, says Christ. Can we, therefore, doubt in the least that his great works of love will remain unrewarded? No, far from it. We have every reason to believe that he has received the reward put aside by God for His faithful servants; that the works of mercy, which will weigh so heavily in our favor on the day of reckoning, done by him so extensively, have merited for him a share in the everlasting bliss of heaven.

In conclusion, I offer my sincerest sympathy to the relatives and friends of our departed. First of all, of course, to his sorrowful and bereaved widow. A firm bond has been severed; a great void has been made in a loving heart. Although we, my friends, deplore sincerely his departure out of this life and feel his loss keenly, the one upon whom the blow falls most heavily is she who is left lonely and desolate to mourn the death of her beloved husband. Weep; there is every reason for you to weep, but through your tears look meekly to the God of all consolation, and He who has inflicted the wound will also give the balm to heal it. He will give you strength to bear your cross with patience and resignation to His holy will. In the second place come the children. Children, remember that you are the offspring of a great man, a man of noble character. Imitate your father in the good he has done. Honor him ever after he has gone. Be dutiful children to your mother and thereby you will fulfill the wish of your father. In your conduct and daily life show yourselves worthy descendents of so great a father.

And you, my friends, who have come here this evening to pay your last tribute of respect and love to our departed friend, do not forget him when the cold earth shall have covered his remains.

Honor him always in time to come. Try to become as great and useful a citizen as he was; imitate him in all he has done for the good of the community. Let us all remember him in our prayers, that God may give him eternal rest and that on the other side of time's vast ocean he may wear forever the crown of everlasting bliss.

References

Amarillo Sunday Globe News Library, as taken from the *Daily Times Herald*, Dallas, Texas. Included in the files of Temple Lea Houston.

DATE DUE